GUARDIAN ANGEL

GUARDIAN ANGEL

Edee Smaldone Corrias

ISBN-13: 9781973805779
ISBN-10: 1973805774

11/22/2014

11/22/2014

Acknowledgements

Thank you to my loving husband, Pete, whose encouragement is priceless. Thank you to my wonderful writing partners at the two Abacoa Writers' Groups. Your support and critique continues to advance me to become a better writer. Many thanks to Mary Freeland; she gave me the idea of a Guardian ad Litem when I struggled with the idea of Becca attending school as an undercover. A special thank you to Judy Ratto, my editor and friend. Her knowledge and support helped turn this book into a readable novel. My thanks to all those who believe in me and encouraged me to continue to write. And thank you to Becca's parents, Terri Lankton and Doug Brown, who allowed me to have their beautiful daughter's picture on the cover, and use Becca's name as the heroin in this novel.

When day is done,
the lights are dim.
A voice rings softly
in my ear.
I listen,
as thoughts are clear.
In another direction
I follow your lead.
A new book is formed,
Indeed!

-EDEE SMALDONE CORRIAS

PROLOGUE

OFFICER JASON REGINO LEARNED FIRST-HAND about teenage suicide when he was a rookie on the police force. He sat straight in his seat and began to tell Becca and Eric about Susie, a freshman new to high school.

Susie didn't have many friends and wanted to belong, so she befriended some freshman girls who were also trying to belong. They met in the cafeteria every day to discuss how they could meet boys. At first, Susie thought it was great that she had some cool friends.

A small group of sophomore girls gathered in a cluster where boys were usually hanging around. They wore lots of makeup and tight, short skirts. Some had tattoos, body piercing, and hair streaked with blue, purple, and pink.

The sophomores began to make fun of Susie and her friends, pointing at them, laughing at *their* hair and clothes. Because Susie was quiet, she was singled out. They called her names, bad names, whore, slut, dirt bag, and porky. Susie was none of these. She was extremely shy, and didn't stick up for herself. Her own friends started calling her names too and wouldn't sit with her at lunch. They were glad the others weren't picking on them.

The lunchtime taunts escalated into cyber bullying. Every day there was another lie about her on the internet, and every day she became more despondent. Her mother tried to talk to her, but she would shut down and stay in her room. This went on for weeks. Susie lost weight and looked as though she hadn't slept. Then her grades slipped. A's dropped to B's and eventually she was coming home with C's and D's. Her mother thought she might be taking drugs and accused her one day. Susie looked at her mother and said, "Even you?"

At first her mother didn't know what she was talking about until one day she went into her room to tidy up and saw her computer logged onto her Facebook page. Desperate, she wanted to know what was happening to her daughter. She began clicking through the pages. What she saw horrified her.

But it was too late. Susie took her life two days later.

C H A P T E R   1

———◆———

Monday
April 11, 2016

ROWDY HIGH SCHOOL STUDENTS FILLED the cafeteria. They shouted, threw things, used profanity, and texted on their cell phones. A female police officer walked around, trying to keep order.

Dylan Baker and his "crew" sat at one of the tables, adding to the frenzy. Three of the boys, Dylan, Ryan, and Ethan were seniors. Tony Sorvino and two girls, Lorraine and Tessa, were juniors. Tony and Ethan were throwing French fries at the girls.

"Stop that Tony," yelled Tessa. "That shit is going in my hair, I swear you're turnt."

Tony laughed. "Look, I added another color."

Tessa's blonde hair, with shades of pink running through it, was cut short, exposing a scorpion tattoo on her neck. A rebellious outcast, Tessa appeared

1

older and wiser than her years. Other than her association with this group, her underlying cruel and devious persona made it difficult to keep friends. She flicked the food loose, threw it back at Tony, and cursed.

"Yeah, Ethan, yours went down my shirt," said Lorraine, a tall brunette with long hair and hazel eyes. One of her eyebrows was pierced with a shiny gold stud.

"Ooh," said Ethan, "don't ya know food helps them grow."

"They're fine," said Lorraine, picking at her top as she looked at Dylan for approval. Her low cut, tight-fitting tee enhanced her seductive body. Lorraine was a follower. She wanted to be liked, especially by Dylan, who she considered their leader.

They laughed and joked. It all seemed innocent until Ethan said, "Hey, Dylan, there's that rachet-ass girl who likes to cut up frogs in biology class. Let's have some fun with her."

Dylan was the brooding type, always on the verge of anger. The other boys knew this and avoided making him mad. Because his last name was Baker, a boy once teased him and said, "Hey, Dylan, time to make the donuts." The next day that boy came to school with a black eye, his arm in a sling, and walking with a limp. From that day on, no one ever teased him again, especially about his name.

Dylan looked over at the girl sitting alone eating her lunch and reading a book. Without a word, he took out his phone and started texting.

Lorraine, obsessed with Dylan, was jealous of any girl he paid attention to, even if it was negative. "Who are you texting?"

The look he gave her said it all. He narrowed his eyes and glared. She shook her head and turned away.

At the other table sat Kelly, a petite, shy, and studious sixteen-year-old sophomore with dark, wavy hair tied in a ponytail. Her fair complexion complemented her large brown eyes. She always received good grades in all her classes. When her phone chirped, she picked it up and read the text. She gasped, put her hand to her mouth, and looked around the room. Without finishing her lunch, she grabbed her things and rose from the table.

Dylan nodded to Ethan, who looked up and saw Kelly leaving. Immediately, he knew what to do. Making sure the police officer was not watching, he darted over to her and grabbed her arm. "Hey, where are you going, ho? You didn't finish your lunch." He flicked her ponytail, pulled her close to his chest, and rubbed against her. "Don't you look cute today? Come and join us." He pointed to his table.

Several of the students from adjacent tables were observing. It was clear she was an object of bullying, and because she was targeted, no one wanted to sit with her.

Frightened, with her face distorted, Kelly pleadingly glanced around the room for help. Some of the students looked, then turned away, grateful it wasn't one of them.

———•———

A sophomore, Michael James, sat at another table and watched. He was in several of Kelly's classes and knew how shy and sensitive she was. At one point, he half stood, then thought better of it and sat back down. He had been bullied many times by Dylan's posse. He was especially afraid of Dylan, who he knew was capable of physical harm. His reputation was well known.

Michael could see that Kelly was terrified and didn't want to have anything to do with the students at Dylan's table. He wished in his heart that he could help her, but he was as frightened as she was.

———•———

Ethan held onto Kelly's arm and pulled. She resisted as tears welled in her eyes. He continued to laugh and tug at her. Managing to drag her to their table, he shoved her down in the empty chair next to Dylan.

"Please, please," Kelly whispered. Tears streamed down her face, and she shook uncontrollably.

"Pleeeez, pleeez," Dylan mocked. "Please what?" His stare was devious. "Why are you still around? We thought you would kill yourself by now."

He grabbed her arm, glanced around to see that none of the teachers or the police officer was watching. Fortunately, the officer was on the other side of the room settling another rowdy dispute.

Kelly was so scared; she swayed and almost passed out. When the others saw this, they all began to laugh.

Lorraine didn't appear to care that they were picking on Kelly. She was only concerned that Dylan was paying attention to her. "This freakin' skank is a bitch. She doesn't deserve to sit here with us. I can't breathe with her around. Why doesn't she die already?"

"Yeah, you're right." Dylan shoved her. "Get the hell outta here."

Kelly got up and ran out of the lunchroom, crying.

Ryan shouted, "Bye-bye, Froggie. Check you later."

They all laughed.

Ethan jutted his jaw. "She's in my biology class, Dylan. I'll have some fun with her later."

C H A P T E R   2

Five days earlier
Wednesday
April 06, 2016

Rebecca Rose Curtis, lovingly known as Becca, raced through the streets in her shiny red Kia Optima. She was late for the funeral of Jacob Jefferies, one of the partners at, Hawkins, Loyola and Jefferies, the personal injury law firm where she worked. They let everyone leave early for the service, but she was delayed with a phone call from an irate client. Part of her job as a legal secretary was to listen to the client's questions and try to answer them before transferring to one of the attorneys.

Why is there so much traffic at this time of the morning? C'mon, lady, move your butt. Are you sightseeing? Becca didn't want to be late. Slim, five-foot-five with long blonde hair and big blue eyes, she was quite a beauty.

At twenty-three years old, she was very levelheaded, efficient in her job, and responsible in her life. Still living at home with her parents and going to law school at night to pass the bar, she had hoped that one day she would work for the firm as an attorney. Mr. Jefferies, whom she liked and admired, had encouraged her. He would always say, "Becca, I like your spirit. You're going to be a great lawyer one day."

She was anxious to make the service before the eulogy was read. *I'm sure there are so many nice things that can be said about him. He was always kind to me, and patient when I didn't understand something. I'm gonna miss you, Mr. Jefferies.* He helped her learn so much about the law.

Whew, I made it. Becca parked the car in St. Ann's parking lot. She rushed into the church. The organ music was playing one of her favorite songs, *Amazing Grace.* She sat in a back row seat so as not to disturb anyone. She was thinking how different a Baptist ceremony was from Catholic. The Catholics were so solemn, while the Baptists were joyful. She preferred the latter. But today, it was solemn.

After the song was over, Mr. Jefferies' son Eric, who also worked at the firm as a young attorney, got up to speak.

Okay, now let's hear it. Becca sat back in her seat to listen to some wonderful attributes. Eric read from a paper.

Now why would you have to read from a paper? Didn't you know your dad? Can't you talk from your heart?

Eric Jefferies started to say that he was a wonderful father, a better husband, a good attorney, and lived a wholesome life. He said, "While my father was alive, he helped many people as an attorney. He is going to be missed at the firm and certainly missed at home. Rest in peace, Dad." Then he stepped down and went back to his seat.

Becca sat with her mouth open. *Is that all he can say about a man who raised him and taught him all he knew about being a good lawyer? Maybe he was nervous.*

The priest got up to speak and repeated almost the same things. The service continued with the liturgy and more singing. At the end of the service, everyone began filing out of the church. Becca sat for a few moments thinking of what she would have said about Mr. Jefferies with only the little knowledge she had of him from the office. It would have been much, much more than what his son had said.

After most of the people were out, she got up and walked to her car. There was a luncheon held at a local restaurant following the ceremony. Becca was invited along with all the other office members. Mr. Jefferies was cremated several days before, and his ashes were spread in the ocean where he loved to fish.

Becca had so much work to do at the office. Since it was lunchtime, and she was hungry, she decided to attend the luncheon.

Most of the office workers were there. She tried to sit as close to the family members as she could. She wanted to talk to his son about the eulogy. She wanted to ask Eric why he was nervous since he was a trial attorney and fought in court on many cases.

She managed a seat opposite Eric. Everyone engaged in small talk, some laughing, while Mrs. Jefferies patted her eyes several times. She couldn't hold back the tears.

How sad, she must have loved him. I know she'll miss him. She loved to fish with him too. Her daughter was sitting next to her and occasionally put her arm around her mother.

Becca observed. This was her second funeral service. The first was for her grandmother, who died last year.

She had some small talk with those around her, and then she addressed Eric. "I see you were nervous during the eulogy."

"No I wasn't. What makes you say that?"

"Well, you didn't go into detail. I thought your father was a great man. I would have a lot more to say about him." Becca was now adamant.

He looked around, leaned over the table, and whispered, "You're out of line, Curtis. That's the way it's done in our church."

She leaned over the table and whispered, "What does it matter which church? A good man is a good man, and all should know."

He shook his head, indicating the conversation was over. Becca raised her eyebrows and gave him a look that said, *"Really?"* She made a mental note to discuss this again back at the office.

If my father died, they would have to drag me from that podium. I would let the world know how much we loved and admired him for all the good things he stood for. I would be fair; I would even mention some of the bad things, not that there were many, only a few. Becca got a stabbing pain in her heart at the thought of her father's passing. Up until now, this was the first time she had ever thought of it. *I must ask him, as well as my mother, how they're feeling. I really take them for granted.*

C H A P T E R   3

BECAUSE BECCA HAD A LOT of work to do, she decided to go back to the office. Only a few people were left working. Most had gone to the funeral service, and then probably went home. Her cubicle was in a corner opposite Mr. Jefferies' office, which allowed her some small level of privacy.

As she was busy working, she heard a light tapping on the outside of her cubicle. She looked up to see Eric Jefferies peeking around the wall. Eric, a six-foot twenty-eight-year-old, had sandy blond hair and blue eyes. Becca thought he was cute and looked a lot like his mother. Mr. Jefferies had been shorter with dark hair.

"I see you came back to work, Curtis. You know you could have taken the afternoon off. No one expected the employees to come back."

"Yes, I know. But I had so much work to do, so I thought I'd come back and finish up."

"By the way, what was all that nonsense at the restaurant?" Eric said, in an irritated voice.

"Your father was such a wonderful man. I just thought you would have said a little more about him. There was certainly a lot more you could have said."

"I respected my father tremendously. You know that. But our church gave us previous orders not to let the eulogy go beyond ten minutes."

"Why?"

"Are you Catholic, Becca?"

"Baptist."

"Well, some Catholic churches are like that. Some give you as much time as you need, allowing others to come up as well. Unfortunately, our church had a time restraint. There was another memorial service."

"Oh, I'm sorry, Eric, I didn't know." Becca's saddened look matched her apology.

"It's okay. I didn't want to get into it at the restaurant. My mom is taking it pretty hard. They were very close and spent most of his free time together." He jutted his head towards her desk. "What are you working on that's so important?"

"Actually they are pleadings for agreeable orders that your dad and I were working on last week. By the way, who'll take his place?"

"I'm not sure? Frank Harris spoke to me yesterday. He thinks I may take over my father's practice, since I worked closely with him and knew the projects he was working on."

"Oh, so that will make you *my* boss." Becca had a slight smile on her face. It was obvious she was teasing him. "Since your father was a partner, do you think they'll make *you* partner?"

"Oh, now you're getting carried away. That won't happen for a long time, if it ever happens."

Becca let out a sigh, looked down then up at him. "You're a good lawyer, Eric, but how do we replace your father?"

"I'm not even going to try, but I'm gonna give it one helluva run."

They both laughed. Becca put her hand over her mouth. She didn't want anyone to hear their laughter even though there were only several people left in the office.

"Hey, Eric, I'm sorry if I upset you at lunch. Sometimes my mouth speaks before my brain gets a chance to catch up."

Eric smiled. "If you want to be a trial lawyer, you better control that."

"Oh, from your mouth to God's ears. I'm working so hard going to school at night and here in the daytime. I have at least a year before I take the Bar. Your dad was so helpful to me. When I had a problem, he always made time for me. I'm really going to miss him."

"Well, you know, it's only been two years since I passed the Bar. I think I can help you." Blushing, he said, "That is, if you want my help."

"Gee thanks, Eric, I'm sure I'm gonna need all the help I can get."

They chatted a little more about his father. Eric told her other wonderful things she didn't know about him. It made her respect his father more.

"It's terrible that the Church didn't let you tell your story. You have so many wonderful memories."

"Yeah, I'm sorry I couldn't. But everyone knew he was a great guy. Since you wanted to know more, I'm glad I had the chance to tell you. It does make me feel better. I'm going to miss him at home, and especially in the office."

Becca noticed that Eric appeared relaxed while he was relaying stories about his father. *It's good for him to talk. It will help with his mourning.*

"Remember, you're gonna have to help your mom and sister at home."

"Oh yeah, I know that. I promise I will. Speaking of help, do you want me to look over those petitions?"

"I don't want to take up your time, especially today. Maybe you can help in a few days?"

"Okay, I better get going. I'll see you tomorrow."

She lifted her hand and waved. "Bye, Eric. Have a good evening."

After he left, she looked down at her work but couldn't concentrate. She thought what a fool she was to attack Eric in the restaurant. When he came back to the office, she was happy to have the chance to apologize. He was right, if she wanted to be a trial lawyer, she had to think first before speaking. It was important to be controlled. Telling people whatever was on her mind was a bad habit. But then again, that was something Mr. Jefferies liked about her. He always said it was part of her charm.

She was winding down and getting ready to leave the office when Frank Harris, the office manager, tapped on her cubicle.

"Are you ready to leave? I want to lock up."

"Oh, yes, I shut down my computer. Is everyone gone?"

"Yes, it's just us two."

Becca was clearing her desk and reaching for her purse as she spoke to Frank. "I'm ready. I'll walk out with you. I'm really going to miss Mr. Jefferies. Who do you think will take his place?"

Becca didn't let on that earlier Eric indicated he might take over his father's practice, according to Frank.

"I think it will be Eric. But the partners will have to decide."

She liked the idea of working closely with Eric. He was very kind, like his father, and had a good head for the law. She could learn a lot from him.

"I think Eric is a good choice. Who better to take over his father's work?"

"Yes, I agree," said Frank sadly. Good old Jacob Jefferies."

They walked together to the parking lot.

"See you tomorrow, Frank. Have a good evening."

"Thanks, and you do the same, Becca."

She got into her car and sat for a minute before turning on the ignition. Happy she didn't have to go to school this evening. One of the advantages of living at home with her parents was having a home-cooked dinner waiting for her. She was so grateful to be living at home. How could she work, cook, and go to school? *Thanks, Mom and Dad.*

On her way home, she thought of Mr. Jefferies. He was in the office one day and gone the next. He had a massive heart attack and died that same day. Never recovering, never having the time to say good-bye to his family. He was only fifty-nine years old. Becca's father was fifty-eight. This made her aware of the vulnerability of life. *Wow, life is short!*

She was tired and looked forward to having one of her mother's delicious meals. But most of all, she was going to let her parents know how much they meant to her.

—◆—

CHAPTER 4

"MMM, WHAT'S FOR DINNER, MOM?" Becca said, walking in the door and breathing in the delicious aroma.

Becca's mother, a graying fifty-five-year-old spoke from the kitchen. "It's pasta and meatballs. I made it for your father and me. Don't worry. I made you salmon and broccoli. I know you always want to eat healthy."

Walls painted in a soft yellow, the kitchen was warm and cozy. The large bay window in front of the sink made it pleasant in the morning sun. It was spacious with a working island in the middle. The counter, with five seats, divided the kitchen from the dining room.

"Okay, Mom, you got me. That pasta smells heavenly, I may try some." Becca walked into the kitchen and kissed her mother. "Hello. Since when do you cook Italian?"

"Dad played golf with an Italian friend last week. He bragged about his wife's cooking. So Dad asked for a recipe. He gave it to him the other day. We both went to buy the ingredients, and I decided to give it a try. It really tastes great."

"Have you had your dinner yet?" Becca asked.

"Yes, we did. We thought you would be late, so we went ahead."

"Oh, that's fine. Yes, I went back to the office after the service."

Her mother was busy in the kitchen. "Are you ready to eat? I kept it warm for you." She took Becca's dinner out of the oven.

"Yes, I'm starving, and your pasta smells so good."

Her dad, a short balding man, walked into the kitchen. "Hello there."

"Hey, Dad, great recipe, smells wonderful." Becca walked over and gave her dad a hug and a kiss.

"How was the service?" he asked.

Becca washed her hands at the kitchen sink, something she did ever since she was a little girl. "Dad, it was strange." She dried her hands and sat down at the counter.

"Strange? What do you mean?"

Her mother placed her dinner on the counter in front of her.

"Well, I was ready for a banging eulogy."

Her mother looked at her and frowned at her use of words describing the eulogy.

"You know how all of us talked about Grandmom at her service?" Becca said. "We couldn't stop talking about her. Eric Jefferies gave his father's eulogy and spoke for only a few minutes, barely touching on what a wonderful man he was. He told me later that the priest told him to keep it at a minimum because there was another service following theirs." Becca picked up her fork and knife and started eating the salmon. "Mmm, this is good, Mom."

"Thanks, dear," said her mother. "Oh, that's too bad about the eulogy. I know how much you cared about Mr. Jefferies."

Her father shook his head. "That's really strange. How do you stop your heart from talking?"

"I know, right? Later at the office, Eric actually gave me the eulogy he wanted to give at the service, and told me some wonderful things about his father. I think he enjoyed telling me. It was his way of giving a true eulogy."

"Who's going to take his place?" her father asked.

"I believe it will be Eric. The office manager told Eric and me that he thought it might be him, but it was up to the partners. I hope they make up their mind real soon, because there are some loose ends that Mr. Jefferies left, and I need direction."

"I'm sure they'll decide soon. After all, it is a flourishing law firm," her father said.

"Yeah." Becca kept eating.

"Are you enjoying that?" her mother asked.

"Oh yes, delicious."

"Wait until you taste the pasta," her mother said.

"I can't wait. Hey, Dad, how's the tooth fairy business?" Her father was a children's orthodontist, and since Becca was little, always referred to his practice as *the tooth fairy business.* He often had to pull teeth to make room for the overbites. Before he would pull the tooth, he told the child, "I need to save this for the tooth fairy." After the tooth was pulled, he'd tell his assistant to put the tooth in the top drawer of a little cabinet in the front office. When he was finished, he would walk the child out, open the draw, and the tooth would be gone. In its place was a crisp one-dollar bill. Her father then told the child that the tooth fairy paid a visit while he was working on their braces. What the child didn't know was that his assistant had put the tooth in another draw and placed the dollar bill into the top drawer. He always had a stash of crisp dollar bills for just that occasion.

"It's great. Little Mary Jones asked for bright green rubber bands to match her outfit. When I asked her what she does when she changes her outfit, she said, 'change the rubber bands.' I had to go searching for all different colors for her. She wanted red wires, I drew the line."

"You wouldn't let me get away with that when I was young."

"Times have changed, sweetie."

Becca shook her head while she continued eating. "You know some parents kick their kids out when they graduate college or turn twenty-one. I'm so glad you two let me continue to live here so I can get my law degree."

"It's our pleasure. We're so glad we can help in your career," her father said.

"Of course, dear," said her mother. "We're delighted you're here. I enjoy cooking for you. I get pleasure seeing you enjoy it."

Becca was almost done eating. She thought about today and felt sadness. The service made her think that someday she may have to prepare a eulogy for her parents. She put it in the back of her mind but knew she would have many, many wonderful things to say about both of them.

"You look dreamy. Are you thinking of the funeral service?"

Becca blinked and looked at her mother. *Oh my goodness, she has always been able to read my mind.* "Yes, I guess I am."

"Don't worry, they'll find a replacement and things will be back to normal," her father said.

"I hope so. I'm not a lawyer yet, so I need help."

Becca got up to clear her dish. Her mother was clearing away the pasta leftovers. They worked together. She liked helping her mother in the kitchen.

"Maybe you'll have some tomorrow."

"I would love to try it. It will be my monthly sinful pleasure." Becca tried to eat as healthy as she could to keep her weight in check. She always indulged in something sinful once a month.

"Okay, your dad and I will join you. At our age, we're entitled to two monthly sinful pleasures, some-times three."

That made Becca uncomfortable. She thought, once again, of her parents' mortality, and how short life really is. *We're so busy working to get ahead, and then one day it all stops. Poor Mr. Jefferies.*

"Hey, Mom, how about letting me finish clearing the kitchen. You go in the living room and relax with Dad."

"Oh that's okay, dear. He's going to watch that crazy TV show with all the serial killers."

"It's a great show," her father said. "It shows you the inner minds of people who have psychological issues. I enjoy how the agents profile the criminals. I should've been a cop."

"Dad, you would have excelled no matter what career you chose." Becca smiled and hugged her dad.

"Oh, it's great to know your kid really admires you," he said jokingly.

Becca knew that deep down he really meant it. She had nothing but admiration for both her parents. She was their only child. Because of her mother's conception issues, the doctors thought she would never be able to conceive. They felt so blessed when Becca arrived. When Becca was in high school, her friends would complain about their parents and actually say they hated them. Becca couldn't understand that. Her parents were always fair and kind. When she did something wrong, they sat her down and explained why she shouldn't have done what she did, and why. Having so much patience, they never yelled or sent her to her room. They always explained everything and made her think of the consequences of her actions.

"Okay, Dad, go watch the serial killers. Mom and I will finish up. Then I want to do some of my school work."

"Too bad you didn't want to become a dentist. I could have helped you with that. Don't stay up too late. Tomorrow morning comes quickly."

"I won't. Thanks, Dad."

"Becca, if you want to study, I can finish up."

"That's okay, Mom, I need to earn my keep." Working in the kitchen helped her unwind and talk about the day. Her mother was a great listener.

They continued working together. "Mom, how's your knee? You said it was bothering you last week." Becca was trying to make mental notes to pay more attention to the ailments of her parents.

"It's feeling a little better. Thanks for asking."

"I guess you and Dad can go dancing again." They both laughed. Her father was a wonderful man, but a lousy dancer.

C H A P T E R   5

FIVE DAYS PASSED BEFORE BECCA received the news that Eric would be taking over Mr. Jefferies' cases. She was relieved. A few of the other attorneys were helping her with the pending cases, but things started to get mixed up. The work was being duplicated, putting more pressure on Becca.

A memo was sent out that Jacob Jefferies' cases were now being assumed by Eric, and that Becca would be working as his assistant. Before the memo came out, Eric was one of the lawyers helping her. She found it easy to work with him. The duplication occurred when several of the other attorneys stepped in. Although she appreciated their help, in the long run, it created havoc.

Today Eric moved into his father's office. It was conveniently across from Becca's cubicle. She could see him bringing in his boxes. His office had a glass window. The letters J a c o b were being removed and changed to E r i c.

Becca viewed the new progression and sighed. Eric was good in the last few days, helping her with the cases. But that was when he was her fellow worker. Now things were different. He was her *boss*. She wondered if he would treat her as such.

Should I ask if he needs help? No, I don't want to start off on the wrong foot. But that's just being nice… No, I'll wait for him to ask me.

Becca had a pile of pleadings to index. She worked for about an hour trying to catch up and clear her basket. Hearing a tap-tap on the wall of her cubicle, she looked up and saw Eric standing there.

"Hey, Becca, can I bother you for a minute?" She thought he looked lost and a little confused.

"Sure, I was going to ask you if you needed help, but you looked busy moving in." *I should have asked him. Why didn't I pay attention to my instincts?*

"Yeah, it's strange moving into my father's office. I have a lot of mixed feelings."

"I'll bet. What can I help you with?"

"There are some files that need to be prioritized. Since you know the cases, can you help me sort them out? Which one is the most important?"

"Oh, sure. When do you want to do that?"

"How about first thing after lunch?"

"Okay, I'm eating lunch at my desk today. I'm trying to catch up. Just call me when you're ready."

"I'm going over to the sandwich shop. Don't eat at your desk. Why don't you join me?"

"Oh, thanks, but I brought something from home."

"It'll keep. Come on; we'll get a quick bite."

Becca was confused. Now that he was her boss, was it appropriate for her to join him for lunch? "No, you go ahead. I'll see you when you get back."

"No, we both need a break. Clear your mind. We'll be fresh when we get back." He laughed and said, "Remember, I'm your boss now. Seriously, we need a break."

Becca smiled. She looked around at all the paperwork on her desk. "You know what? We do need a break. I'll join you, but only if you let me pay for myself."

"Of course. I got my father's job not his salary."

They both laughed. She shut down her computer and grabbed her purse.

It was a beautiful spring day. They walked down the street to the local sandwich shop. They each ordered a sandwich and sat at one of the outside tables. He did try to pay, but she refused.

"I usually get a salad, but the tuna on rye that you ordered really looked good," said Becca.

"It is. Wait until you taste it. They make the best tuna. What did you bring from home that you'll be missing?"

"A salad. I'll probably eat it for dinner."

Eric was right; Becca loved the tuna. "This is great."

"I told you. I would never lie."

They talked about the cases while Becca brought him up to date. At first, when he asked her to go to lunch, she misread the invitation. She thought he might have a *thing* for her, and that wouldn't be a bad thing. But seeing his enthusiasm about the cases, she realized he wanted to catch up. Feeling a tug at her heart, she wondered what it would be like if he did have a thing for her.

CHAPTER 6

BECCA AND ERIC FINISHED THEIR lunch and headed back to the office. She was glad he invited her. He was right. She needed a break.

Becca liked Eric. She enjoyed working with him. He was always polite, smart, and didn't act like a boss; he still treated her like a co-worker. As the son of one of the partners, Eric never took advantage of his position. Unlike Luke Hawkins, another attorney and son of one of the partners, who was a slacker and a flirt. Luke expected everyone to treat him as royalty. Becca didn't care for him. He always passed the buck and wanted everyone to do his job. Treating her as an equal, Eric never made her feel that he was better than she. Becca was glad when Eric was chosen to take his father's position and equally glad that she was selected to be his secretary, as she had been for his father.

The rest of the day went by quickly. At four o'clock, they were still busy working on the cases.

While she was deep in thought, her phone rang. She picked it up on the third ring. Susan, the receptionist, was on the other end.

"Becca, I think this is a case for Mr. Jefferies."

"Mr. Jefferies? Oh, Eric. Yes, I'll take it," said Becca. "Good afternoon, Mr. Jefferies' office, Becca speaking."

The caller seemed nervous. "Yes, yes can I speak to him?"

"Yes, certainly, may I tell him whose calling?"

"My name is Ann Richards."

"What is it in reference to Ms. Richards?"

"Please let me speak to him, it's urgent," she begged.

Usually Becca tried to get some information from a client before she forwarded the call, but the tone and urgency in the woman's voice made Becca ring through to Eric.

"Eric, there's an Ann Richards on the line. She says it's urgent. She sounds desperate."

"Put her on."

Becca forwarded the call to Eric. She looked through the glass door to see the expression on Eric's face when he spoke to her. He was shaking his head as he picked up his pen to jot something down. Becca turned and went back to work.

Eric talked to the lady for about twenty minutes. When he finished, he stood, walked over to the window, and looked out for several minutes. He then went over to his phone and rang Becca. "I just got off the phone with Mrs. Richards."

"Wow." Becca looked at the time on her computer. "You were on a long time."

Eric was silent for a few seconds then spoke. "Can you come in? I want to discuss the case."

Becca got up and quickly went into his office. He motioned for her to sit.

Eric paced the room deep in thought. Like his father did before he would talk about a case, Eric walked back and forth with his hand on his chin. Becca recognized this and waited. After a long minute, he stopped pacing, sat down, and spoke. "Her child is being bullied at school. Mrs. Richards is afraid her daughter may commit suicide. She wants to sue the kids that are bullying her."

"Really? I don't think your father ever had a case about bullying."

"I don't think so either."

He proceeded to discuss the case with Becca. "Ann Richard's daughter, Kelly, is a sixteen-year-old high school junior. Her mother described her as sweet, smart, and socially introverted. She's being bullied by her peers because she doesn't want to conform to their ways. As she described it, there is a group of kids who are out of control with drugs, body piercings, and sex. They started teasing Kelly at the beginning of the school year and asked her to join them at night to party. When Kelly refused, they began to taunt her. One of the boys rubbed up against her at her locker. She froze and didn't know what to say. When the boy saw her reaction, he knew he could take advantage of her. He told the others and, in turn, each of them teased and made fun of her. They cursed at her and sent horrible text messages. They posted nasty things on Facebook, saying she was worthless and ugly."

Becca was speechless and kept shaking her head as Eric continued.

"Today, Kelly came home crying, and told her mother everything. The bullies accosted her in the cafeteria, and no one helped. In the last few weeks, Kelly went from a being a happy teenager to a sullen, quiet, withdrawn girl.

"Her mother was so distraught because while Kelly told her about today, she said over and over, 'I just want to die. I just want to die.' That's why Mrs. Richards called today. She's terrified, and wants the bullying to stop before her daughter takes her life. The mother said they cyber abused her, sending messages out to all their friends that she was a fat slut. Because they were sending her such terrible text messages, her mother took her phone and arranged to get her another with a new number for her to call in case of an emergency."

"These kids are horrible," said Becca. "I can remember some bullying when I was in high school. But if someone called you a name, it wasn't published on the internet as it is today. I read about incidents in the news and see it on TV. So what are you going to do? Can she sue the kids?"

"She can't sue the kids; she can sue the parents. But first, I have to investigate the situation and make sure she isn't exaggerating. I need to meet with her. By the way, I made an appointment for both of them to come in tomorrow."

"Okay, I'll put it on your calendar." Becca jotted a note on her pad then glanced up at Eric. He had a far-away look on his face. "What are you thinking about?"

"This is a very delicate case. If it's true that she is being bullied, she may very well take her life. I want you to be closely involved in this case. When she comes in, let's pay strict attention to her body language. We should brainstorm and try to ask her as many questions to get to the bottom of the situation. Of course, we have to have proof of the bullying. You asked me what I was thinking about? A Guardian ad Litem."

"Did you know I was a Guardian ad Litem?" said Becca. "Your father had a case where a couple were getting a divorce, and had a minor child. He petitioned the court for an order to appoint me as Guardian ad Litem to investigate what solutions would be in the best interest of the child."

"When was this?"

"A few months ago."

"What happened?"

"I was lucky. They were loving parents. Even though they couldn't stand each other, they didn't let that interfere with the love and care they gave their child. I gave the court a favorable review."

Eric had a smile on his face. "That's our answer. I spoke to Mrs. Richards about a Guardian ad Litem for Kelly, one that would accompany her to her classes and assess the bullying. I'm going to petition the court for an order for you to be her GAL."

Becca had many thoughts swimming in her head, but she liked the idea. Being Kelly's GAL and following her in school was different from the last case. *This girl's life is at stake.* She knew bullying was rampant in teenage society these days and wanted to help. "What will the petition state?"

"That she is believed to be a victim of bullying, allowing you to accompany her to her classes. You will review the attitudes of fellow students, gather information, and report your results to the court. This should help us file a suit." Eric wrote as he spoke.

"This means I have to go back to high school."

Eric stopped writing and looked up at Becca. "Yes."

"When will you do this?"

"As soon as we meet with Mrs. Richards, and she signs an agreement letter." Eric kept talking to Becca as he jotted on his legal pad. He glanced up and said, "I'd like to talk to the local police and find out what they know about bullying in high schools."

"I'll get on that right away." Becca wrote on her pad.

"After we talk to the local police, we then contact her high school to find out their procedure on preventing bullying, and what action they take when they find a child is being bullied."

Becca kept writing. "I'm on it."

Eric checked the time on his cell phone. "It's almost five. This can wait till morning. I know you have a class this evening. Why don't you go and eat your salad and head out."

She glanced at her cell too. "Oh, wow. This day flew by. You remembered my salad, thanks. Our first day together and already we have such an interesting case. I'll research the information first thing tomorrow morning." She stood to leave.

"Good work, Curtis. I think we make a good team." Eric smiled at her.

She shook her head and gave him thumbs up. Even though she missed Mr. Jefferies, she was enjoying working for Eric.

Becca went to the small kitchen to retrieve her salad. She ate it standing up. She never liked the idea of eating at her desk even though some of the other girls did.

While eating her salad, she thought about the case. *This should be interesting. I'm going back to high school? If it helps that girl, I'll try my best. What about my job here? Who'll do my work?* Becca's head was spinning. She was exhausted, and now she had another two hours in school. *I hope all of this pays off.*

CHAPTER 7

———◆———

BECCA WAS GLAD SHE WAS still young. There were some older people in her class who were having a hard time. Even though she was tired from the hectic day, she was still able to absorb the lesson. She loved learning about the law.

While in her car and heading home, Becca started thinking about the girl being bullied. Some preliminary work had to be done for Eric before their meeting with the mother and daughter the next day. Eric made the appointment at three in the afternoon, giving them the morning to prepare.

At home, she was greeted with the wonderful aroma of dinner waiting for her in the kitchen. Her parents were visiting friends, and her mother left it warming in the oven. *How great is it to have the best parents in the world.*

After freshening up, Becca took her dinner out of the oven. It was the leftover pasta and meatballs.

"Well I guess this will have to be my monthly sinful pleasure." She sat down to eat, and devoured the food. *Oh, this is so good. Mental note: marry an Italian!*

———

The next day Becca arrived early. She wanted to get a good start on the research for the upcoming meeting with Mrs. Richards and her daughter. She contacted the school for information on their procedures for dealing with bullying. Of course, when she spoke to the vice principal, she was told they had *zero* tolerance for bullying. The school official explained the procedures for this offense, which included calling in the parents and suspend the individual.

Next on Becca's list, she called the local police. The woman officer who answered the phone said one of their officers was especially knowledgeable on this subject. She could have him dispatched to the law office.

"That won't be necessary. Please have him call me," said Becca.

"It will be easier if he were dispatched," said the officer.

"Alright then, please tell him to come before twelve noon."

When Becca hung up the phone, she typed up some questions to ask the officer. She wanted to know as much as possible before the meeting with Mrs. Richards and her daughter.

Her morning was very busy. Eric was filling his father's shoes nicely. They were becoming a team. Becca enjoyed working for him as much as working for his father. Jacob Jefferies was old school, and Eric was up-to-date law. Both were excellent attorneys.

The receptionist directed another unusual call to Eric's office, a victim of road rage. Becca asked, "Why don't you send the call to Luke Hawkins? He's an ambulance chaser."

"The man really needs someone's help. I think Eric is that person."

"What's going on around here? Is there a full moon?" She made Susan laugh. "Okay, put him through."

The gentleman told Becca his name was Ed Klein.

"Mr. Klein, what can we do for you?" By the sound of his voice, Becca could tell he was elderly, older than her father.

He proceeded to tell his story.

While driving on I-95, in the middle lane and going the speed limit, he realized he had to get off the next exit. He looked in his rear view mirror and right side mirror and saw a vehicle a good distance away. Mr. Klein safely entered the right lane to exit. The car that was a safe distance away suddenly barreled up behind him. It went into the middle lane, passed him, and cut him short in the right lane before he could exit. The driver came upon him so suddenly that it caused Mr. Klein to bump the rear of the offending vehicle. They pulled over on the side of the road to assess the damage and exchange license and insurance—so he thought. A man in his early forties leaped out of his vehicle, cursing profusely, telling the elderly man he shouldn't be driving at his age. When the police came, the younger man told them Mr. Klein hit his vehicle and was liable for damages. Mr. Klein told the police officer that the other man cut him off abruptly, and he had no opportunity to avoid the accident. Since he hit the other car, and there were no witnesses, Mr. Klein received a ticket for reckless driving.

"I'm outraged. I was driving within the speed limit. I did *not* cut that man off. Even though I'm eighty-years old, I have a valid driver's license. I would like to come in and make a suit against the *other* driver for reckless driving."

"Were there any witnesses?" said Becca.

"I'm sure people saw it."

"Did any come to your defense?"

"No, not at the scene," he said sadly.

Becca took his information and made an appointment for next week. From what she knew about driving accidents, you always needed a witness. She made the appointment anyway hoping Eric could help him in some way. Road rage was a real threat. Becca felt sorry for Mr. Klein.

At eleven a.m., Susan rang her phone again.

"Becca, its Officer Jason Regino. He said he has an appointment with you."

Oh yes, the officer who knows about bullying. "Let him sit in the waiting room a minute. I want to tell Eric he's here."

She peeked through the glass door. Eric had his head buried in paperwork. She dialed him. He looked up and saw her looking at him. He picked up the phone.

"That officer is here. Do you want me to send him in?"

"Yes, and I want you to come in too." She hung up and dialed Susan. "You can send the officer in now. Thanks."

Jason Regino was a young twenty-five-year-old police officer. Although young, he had an air of superiority in his walk. He was tall, dark, and handsome. His muscles were bulging through his shirt. It was obvious he spent a lot of time at the gym.

Becca was surprised when he walked in. She expected a seasoned officer. She shook his hand. "Good afternoon." His grip was firm.

Her father always told her to watch out for the limp handshake. "You can tell the character of a man by how he shakes your hand."

Jason Regino raised his eyebrows when she returned a firm hand as well.

"Regino, that's Italian isn't it?" *Hmm, Italian.* Becca was thinking of the great dinner she had last night.

"Yes, ma'am, it is."

Oh no, he ma'amed me. How old does he think I am? I'm probably his age.

"My language in high school was Italian; I believe your last name means 'king'."

Jason pursed his lips and tilted his head. "Not many people know that. I'm impressed."

She led him into Eric's office. Becca introduced him. He shook Eric's hand with the same gusto as he did with her.

"Sit down, Officer. Tell us what you know about bullying," Eric said as he pointed to one of the chairs circling a small conference table.

All three sat down. Becca had her yellow pad ready.

CHAPTER 8

<hr />

JASON REGINO SAT STRAIGHT IN his seat. "Bullying has always been serious among high school students. Because of cyberspace, it has become worse."

Jason then told them about one of his recent experiences.

"I was the officer on call when one of the local high school students committed suicide. She was a fourteen-year-old freshman." He averted his eyes and glanced out the window. Hesitating, he looked down then up at Becca and Eric. He took a deep breath before he continued. "I was a rookie on the force; only one year, and I thought I saw it all: rapes, drugs, homicides. When we went in, the parents were screaming and shaking the girl as if they could wake her from the dead. The girl got hold of some sleeping pills and overdosed."

Becca stopped writing, raised her head, and opened her mouth.

Eric spoke. "Evidently she was being bullied. Can you tell us about that?"

Becca squirmed in her seat, glanced at Jason, and had her pen ready to write.

"Her name was Susie, a freshman, new to the high school. She didn't have many friends and wanted to belong, so she befriended some freshman girls who also tried to belong. They met in the cafeteria every day to discuss how they could meet some of the boys. At first, Susie thought it was great that she had some cool friends." While he spoke, Jason placed both hands on his knees. "At lunchtime, the group of sexy sophomore girls gathered in a cluster. They usually had some boys hanging around."

Eric interrupted. "What do you mean by sexy?"

"You know… lots of makeup, tight, short skirts, and different colored hair."

"What about the dress code? Isn't that inappropriate?" said Eric.

"I would say so, but if the parents let them dress that way, what can the school do?"

"Sorry to interrupt. Continue."

"They started to make fun of Susie and her friends. They pointed at them, laughing at their hair and clothes." Jason shook his head. "For some reason, they singled out Susie. They began calling her names, bad names, whore, slut, dirt bag, and porky. I met Susie before she died. She was none of these. She was extremely shy and didn't stick up for herself.

So even her own friends started calling her names and wouldn't sit with her at lunch. They were glad the sexy girls weren't picking on *them*."

Jason sighed deeply. He raised his hands from his knees and folded his arms across his chest. "Eventually, they started cyberbullying, putting bad things about her on the internet. Every day she came home despondent. Her mother tried to talk to her, but she would shut down and go to her room. This went on for weeks. Susie lost weight and looked as though she hadn't slept. Then her grades slipped. She usually got A's and B's. Now she was coming home with C's and D's. Her mother thought she might be taking drugs and accused her one day. Horrified, Susie looked at her mother and said, 'Even you?'

"At first her mother didn't know what she was talking about until one day she went into her room to tidy up, and saw her computer logged onto her Facebook page. Desperate, she wanted to know what was happening to her daughter. She began clicking through the page. What she saw horrified her. She knew then that her daughter was being bullied."

Becca was mesmerized. Every once in a while she looked up at Eric. He was bent over, hands on his knees, sitting on the edge of his seat, listening.

Jason sat tall in his seat, he never slouched all the while he was there. Occasionally, Becca caught herself and sat up as tall as she could.

Jason continued. "Her mother went to the school with copies of the pages. The principal said he would look into it. One of Susie's old friends saw her mother walk out of the principal's office. The next day he had an assembly warning the children that he would not tolerate bullying of any sort. Her friend knew that Susie's mother was the cause of the assembly. She told the other friends, and they put more pressure on Susie until one day she couldn't take it." His voice cracked slightly.

"You said you met her before she died?" Eric was curious.

"Yes, I did. Before Susie's mother went to the school, she also called the police. I was on call that day and went over to her house to take a report. Susie was so frail; she couldn't talk to me. When I asked her a question, all she could do was shake her head yes or no. That was two days before she died. This happened two months ago, and I told the captain that I wanted to be assigned to all the bullying cases. I want to help. That's why I'm here. If there's another case, I want to be involved."

"Becca, tell Officer Regino what you learned from the school."

She was still in a daze from listening to the officer's report of the case. Blinking a few times, she then referred to her notes. "Of course, they said they have zero tolerance for bullying. When they catch a student who is offending, they issue a suspension. Before the student can return to school, the parent has to speak to the principal. They try to do everything to stop any incidents." Becca looked up from her notes. "Evidently they didn't try hard enough in Susie's case."

"It's so difficult." Officer Regino tried to explain. "The school officials have their hands tied. If the parents don't cooperate, it's hard for them to control the bullying. They can suspend the abusing students, but sometimes there are many and it becomes a problem to suspend them all."

Eric took a deep breath and sat up in his chair. "Since you've had first-hand knowledge of a death due to bullying, in your opinion..." Eric hesitated. "What advice do you have to control this issue?"

"Strictly...in my opinion, I think someone should follow the kid that's being bullied. We have female officers who have been plants in schools. Why, what are you thinking of?"

"Funny you should say that. I was thinking that same thought."

Jason Regino raised his eyebrows and nodded.

"Have you ever heard of a Guardian ad Litem?"

"Yes, I have. Aren't they assigned by the court to check a child's home life?"

Eric nodded. "Yes, but we want to assign one specifically to Kelly to be with her in her class room and observe the bullying."

"These kids are sharp. They won't bully her as long as she has a shadow," said Jason.

"What if they don't know it's a Guardian ad Litem; what if they think it's another student…if she's young enough?" Eric glanced at Becca as he spoke. "Only the officials will know who she is."

Jason turned his head towards Becca. He understood what Eric was suggesting. "You mean her? She'll be the Guardian ad Litem?"

Eric nodded.

Becca turned her head from Eric to Jason. "It's been six years since I was in high school. I don't know if I would know how to act…" She hesitated. "Or look young enough."

Both Jason and Eric spoke in unison. "Yes, you do." Then they both laughed.

Eric stood. It was a cue that the meeting was over. Jason stood as well. Eric reached out to shake the officer's hand. "Thank you for coming in, Officer Regino. We would be happy if you would assist us in this case. You seem to have a handle on the subject."

"Yes, I certainly will do that, and I'll be in touch." He nodded to Becca and shook her hand too. "Thank you, ma'am."

Oh no, he ma'amed me again. But he did say I looked young enough to go back to high school.

She received his firm handshake again. "Thank you for coming, it was very informative."

They both walked out of Eric's office. Jason said goodbye to Becca. She started to walk him out when he said, "That's okay, I know the way out."

Becca couldn't help noticing that he didn't wear a wedding band. *That doesn't mean anything. Some men don't wear them. But he looks like the type that would if he were married.*

She gave a little sigh and thought how dreamy he was, then sat down to continue with her busy schedule.

Her phone rang. It was Eric. "What about that old guy who was involved with road rage?"

"Oh yes, I put that on your calendar, but didn't have time to discuss it before the officer came in. I gave you a little background."

"Yes, it seems the old guy got screwed. It looks like we got two cases of bullying today. Call the local police department where the incident occurred. Find out if a Good Samaritan called to say they saw the accident."

"Great idea. I'll get right on it."

Becca called the police department where the accident happened. She couldn't believe it when the dispatcher said that someone made a report of an accident that seemed to result in road rage. It happened at the same exit and the same time that Mr. Klein described. It was a woman who was driving behind the offender. Her passenger took out her phone and snapped a video of the man crossing the lane and barreling down on the poor unsuspecting driver. She kept the video running, showing the accident was not the old man's fault.

"Please send me the report and the name of the witness. I'm sure our client will be glad to hear about this."

After Becca hung up, she went into Eric's office. "You won't believe what I just found out." She proceeded to tell him about the eyewitness. "You're right, Eric, that poor old guy was being bullied as well. Hopefully, now we can help."

"It was just a hunch when I told you to call the local police department. It always helps to try. That's great news. Let the client know, and set up an appointment for him and the witnesses to come in."

Becca remembered how sad Mr. Klein sounded when telling his story. With an eyewitness and a picture, the other man, the road rage *bully*, would definitely be cited. Maybe even go to jail for reckless driving.

Becca dialed his number. The elderly man answered on the third ring. "Hello, Mr. Klein, this is Becca Curtis from Eric Jefferies' office. I have good news for you."

CHAPTER 9

MR. KLEIN WAS DELIGHTED TO hear that an eyewitness came forward. He didn't think, "in this day and age," that there were any decent people left. Becca said she would make a new appointment for him and the witnesses. "I'll call you as soon as I confirm the date."

"Oh, thank you, miss, thank you. I'm so happy that justice will be done. I'm a good driver, and I want to keep my record as such. Please call me."

"I definitely will, Mr. Klein. You have a great day."

"I will *now*. Thank you." He hung up.

Becca was exhilarated. She was so happy that Mr. Klein was going to get his record cleared. *We're gonna throw the book at that other guy. He should take a course in anger management. What a great idea Eric had to call the local police department. I know his father would be very proud of him.*

When she received the report, name, and number of the witness, she called and made an appointment for her and her passenger to come in with Mr. Klein. Happily, the witness agreed to come in and bring her friend and, of course, the video.

After she called Mr. Klein to confirm the date, she sat back in her chair to go over the events of the day. It had been busy. With a sigh, she took out her notes on the new bullying case and typed them into the file. The clients were coming that afternoon. While she was typing, she suddenly realized she would be out of the office while she was Kelly's GAL. She needed to go over this with Eric. How long would she be in school? What about her job? What about her night classes?

Eric came out of his office and tapped on her cubicle. It was his way of letting her know he was there. He never barged in and started talking. He was always very polite and a wonderful gentleman. She looked up and saw him smiling.

"Hi, can I help you?"

"I can't believe you don't know it's twelve-thirty. I thought *I* was a workaholic. What about lunch?"

She looked at the time on her computer. "Wow, this day is flying by. I never got a chance to ask you what will happen in the office when I go to school as Kelly's GAL."

"Don't worry; we'll talk about it after our meeting with Mrs. Richards and her daughter. By the way, are you going to class tonight?"

Becca sighed. "No, thank goodness, not tonight."

"Good. I'm glad you're passionate about this. I am too. My heart goes out to those poor victimized kids, as well as Mr. Klein. You should get some lunch. The Richards are coming in at three. I'm eating lunch at my desk. I've got some work to do." Eric went into his office and shut the door. Usually, he leaves it open when he's not researching a serious case.

Becca went into the break room to eat her lunch. She wanted to be back at her desk by one and only took thirty minutes. She still had some last-minute preparations before the meeting.

When she returned to her desk, the office bustled. Everyone was back from lunch. Lawyers, paralegals, and office workers were all busy. The firm, a very prestigious law office, had many clients.

Joyce, one of the other paralegals who worked for Luke Hawkins, came over with a donut. "I thought you might need this."

"Joyce, you know I try to stay away from sweets."

"Yes, but we all heard about the case today. I know it's hush-hush, but the office is buzzing about a certain someone going back to school."

"Isn't there anything sacred in this office?"

"Not when you're working with a partner's son."

"Who do you mean, Luke or Eric?"

Joyce widened her eyes. "Luke, of course. Eric keeps things close to the chest."

"Thank goodness," Becca said, almost to herself.

"What is that supposed to mean?" Joyce was a nice girl, but Becca had to be careful what she said to her or else it would be all over the office.

"You were comparing him to Luke, so I agreed with you."

"Here, take this anyway." Joyce handed her the donut. "You're gonna need it this afternoon. The sugar helps you stay alert."

"Thanks." Becca took the donut and set it on a paper napkin on her desk. Under no circumstances would she eat that donut. *Maybe, just a bite? Later?*

In the distance, she could hear Luke shouting at Joyce for a donut. Luke was not only loud; he couldn't keep a secret. Because he was not married, he thought he was God's gift to women, and anyone he flirted with should be grateful for his attention. Often, Becca was a recipient. When he did flirt, she'd blink her eyes at him and laugh it off. That seemed to keep him at bay.

While she was typing away, she glanced up to see Luke walking her way. *Oh no, better get the blinkers ready.*

"Curtis, what's Eric up to with the door shut? Can I go in?"

"Sorry, Luke, he's working on a case."

"Yeah, yeah, I know all about it." Luke gave Becca one of his seductive looks. Becca wanted to burst out laughing in his face, but instead she smiled, blinked her eyes and said, "He's very busy, Luke." Then she laughed. She couldn't hold it in. Luke waved his hand and walked away.

Today of all days, Becca didn't want any interruptions. She knew how important this case was and had to do a lot of research. She picked up the phone to call Officer Regino. There were a few questions she needed answered before the meeting.

"One-five." A women's voice answered.

"This is Becca Curtis from the attorneys' office, Hawkins, Loyola and Jefferies.

"Yes, what can I do for you?"

"Can I speak to Officer Regino? Mr. Jefferies and I are working on a case with him."

"Oh yes, that one. He's on patrol; I'll send him a message to call you. Does he have your number?"

"Yes, he does. Thank you so much." She hung up and wrote a note to herself so she wouldn't forget what to ask him. She wanted to know how to get Kelly to open up and confide in her. From what her mother told Eric, she was withdrawn and didn't want to talk to anyone. According to Jason Regino, this was typical.

It was one-thirty when Eric opened his door. She picked up the donut and walked into his office.

"Here, this is from Joyce."

"Is all the woman thinks of is food?" He reached out his hand and accepted it. "Thanks, it should hit the spot. What about you? Did you get one?"

"No, you know I don't eat sweets… that is, daily. It has to be a special occasion."

"I'll have to remember that."

"So how's the case coming along?" Becca asked. "Are you prepared for them?"

"I think…as prepared as I'm ever going to be," said Eric. "I'm going to try to make Kelly as comfortable as possible."

"How are you going to do that?"

"I've been doing some research. Just follow my lead. After we make her comfortable, I'll have you take her in the small conference room where you can try to have her open up to you."

"Oh." Becca frowned. She wasn't sure she could start a conversation with her. She was anxious to talk to Jason Regino first and hoped he'd call before the meeting.

"Don't worry, I have faith in you. I know you'll be able to get her to talk."

"Have you suggested the GAL yet?"

"Not yet. I'll tell them at the meeting. You discuss our plan with Kelly. Tell her even though you're her GAL and the teachers and officials will be informed, you want to pass yourself off as a student. Confide in her."

Becca's thoughts began to swirl in her head. She did have many things to discuss with Kelly. But she wanted to gain her confidence more than anything. She needed Officer Regino to call.

When the phone rang, Becca looked at her watch. It was two-thirty. "This is Becca."

Susan put the call straight through. "Hi, Ms. Curtis, this is Jason Regino."

"Please, Jason, call me Becca." She was picturing him standing or sitting straight up.

"Okay, Becca, what can I do for you?"

"As you know, we're meeting with Mrs. Richards and her daughter, Kelly, at three. I'm so glad you called. I wanted to ask you some questions before we meet with her."

"Of course. What are your questions?"

"After we meet with both of them, Eric wants me to speak privately with Kelly and try to gain her confidence. I need to be very delicate with her." Becca began, biting her lip. She did that when she was nervous. "Do you have any suggestions?"

"As a matter of fact, I do. When you talk to her, it's important to look her in the eye. At first, she'll turn away. Tell her it wasn't long ago that you were a high school student."

Okay, he's acknowledging that I'm young, even though he often calls me ma'am.

Jason continued. "Tell her about some of the things you experienced in high school, even if you have to make things up."

"What do you mean? Lie to her?"

"No, no that's not what I meant. I can't picture you having any problems in high school. I didn't think you had any bullying experiences. I meant, if you heard of any while you were there, or if any of your friends had problems."

"As a matter of fact, I did have some. My father is an orthodontist and kept my braces on longer than usual because I needed extra treatment. The kids called me *wired*. It really upset me. I went home to tell my father to take them off. I didn't care what my teeth looked like. He told me that was the point. If I didn't leave the braces on, the kids might call me worse names because my teeth would not be straight."

"That's what I mean, tell her stories like that. Gain her confidence. You know, your dad was right; you have a beautiful smile."

Becca pictured him smiling with his sparkling teeth. "Thank you. I'll tell her that story and a few others that I remember."

"Yes, it's important for her to feel you're in her boat. Right now, she thinks she's the only one in the world who's being bullied."

"Wow, Jason, you have a lot of knowledge on this subject."

Jason stammered and said, "Miss… uh, Becca, I have to get back to work. Call me if you need any further assistance."

"I hate calling the precinct. Do you have a personal cell number?"

"Yes, I do." Jason proceeded to give Becca his personal number. "I can't answer during work hours, but you can leave me a message, and I'll call you back. Good luck with Kelly."

Becca sat at her desk for a few moments recalling the phone conversation with Jason. She had mixed emotions about their relationship. She wanted to keep it professional, but there was an underlying attraction. She immediately snapped out of her daydream when the phone rang. It was the receptionist telling her that Mrs. Richards and Kelly were there. They were early.

"Tell them to sit a minute. I'll tell Eric and come out to get them."

Eric's office door was opened. She walked in and announced that they were there.

He shuffled some of his papers around "Okay, I'm ready. You can bring them in."

CHAPTER 10

ALTHOUGH MRS. RICHARDS WAS IN her mid-forties, ashen skin and dark circles under her eyes made her appear older. Her disheveled appearance and mismatched outfit expressed her turmoil. She sat wringing her hands as she stared at her daughter. Kelly's ponytail looked as though it had been slept on. Her clothing was wrinkled as well. The two were quite a sight.

As Becca walked over to them, she tried to act normal. She extended her hand to Mrs. Richards. "Hello, I'm Becca Curtis, Mr. Jefferies' assistant."

Mrs. Richards stood up. When Becca shook her hand, she felt it trembling. Kelly didn't look up and sat staring blankly.

Becca didn't want to appear nervous. All of this was new to her. A few weeks ago, she was a legal secretary handling various personal injury cases. Now she was going to high school as a Guardian ad Litem on a case about bullying. It was a daily subject in the news with many kids being affected. She wanted to help but had to admit to herself that she was apprehensive.

She turned to Kelly and gently touched her shoulder. "Hello, I'm Becca, you must be Kelly."

Kelly looked up with unexpressive eyes that seemed to look through Becca instead of at her. Becca wondered if she and Eric could handle this case. She addressed them both. "Will you follow me? Mr. Jefferies is expecting you."

Most in the office knew about this case, and when Becca and the Richards passed each cubicle, some poked out their heads.

Eric stood and shook Mrs. Richard's hand. He nodded to Kelly. "Please sit," he said, indicating the small round table in his office. He signaled to Becca to shut the door.

When Mrs. Richards had called Eric, she told him that Kelly experienced a horrible incident in the cafeteria and didn't want to go back to school. Mrs. Richards was so distraught at hearing this because of the recent stories of children committing suicide due to bullying. She went to the principal to discuss what Kelly had experienced. The principal said she would have the teachers monitor her classes. The offending students would then be suspended or expelled. But until an incident is observed by faculty, there was nothing she could do. That's when Mrs. Richards decided to call Eric.

———◆———

Eric had researched bullying cases all morning. He thought he was prepared. The physical state of both Kelly and her mother shocked him. He knew he had his work cut out for him. Mrs. Richards told him Kelly was an A student before the bullying started and always talked about being a doctor.

"Tell me, Kelly, what do you like to study in school?" Eric was trying to keep the conversation as normal as possible.

Kelly sat at the table with her head lowered. She didn't respond.

Her mother said, "Kelly likes biology. She wants to be a doctor."

Kelly raised her head, looked at her mother then at Eric, and lowered her head again.

"That's wonderful, Kelly. Healthcare is a great profession." He was not getting through to her.

"You know when I was in high school, my worst subject was biology. I hated when I had to dissect a frog. It really upset me. What about you, Kelly?" He smiled. He knew he was reaching.

She glanced up at him and stared. Putting her head back down again, she almost spoke into her chest. "Yeah, most of the kids think it's disgusting." Then she raised her head and looked out the window. "I don't because I want to be able to operate someday." She continued to stare out the window.

"We need good surgeons," said Eric. "I'm sure you'll be a great one someday because you have a passion. My passion is to be a great attorney."

Eric spoke with sincerity. Kelly nodded her head, agreeing with him but still stared out the window.

"Can you tell me more about school? What else is going on?" Eric encouraged Kelly to talk about the bullying.

Tears welled in her eyes and she shook her head.

"Would you like some water?" Eric grabbed one of the small bottles that were on the table and passed it to her. Now the tears fell freely down her cheeks.

Becca handed her a tissue. Kelly took the tissue and dabbed her eyes.

"Kelly, tell Mr. Jefferies what's happening to you in school," said Mrs. Richards.

With that, Kelly started crying. Her body shook uncontrollably. Becca instinctively put her arm on Kelly's shoulder and began to rub her back. "Don't worry, Kelly, we're going to stop that. You're now on eagle's wings."

All three gave Becca a questioning look.

Mrs. Richards said, "Do you mean *legal eagles?*"

Eric was also wondering what his assistant was talking about. He squinted and mouthed, "What?"

Becca realized they didn't understand. "When I was growing up, whenever I had a problem or was worried or frightened, my father told *me* that *I* was on eagle's wings. He was referring to the song." With her hand on Kelly's back, she crouched in front of the younger girl. "When you're on eagle's wings, you're lifted and held in the palm of His hand."

Kelly listened to Becca, and dabbed her eyes. "I remember that song from church."

Becca said, "Every time I feel anxious, I know I'm on eagle's wings secure in the palm of His hand.

"You mean God's hand?" Kelly questioned.

Becca nodded. "Yes," she said and sat back in her chair.

Mrs. Richards had tears in her eyes, and Eric could only nod in approval.

"Yes, Kelly, we're going to stop this terrible thing from happening to you." Eric shuffled some papers in a folder. "Becca is going to be your Guardian ad Litem."

Kelly and Mrs. Richards turned their attention to Eric. "What's that?" Mrs. Richards asked.

"A GAL, as we call it, is a person the court appoints to investigate what solutions would be in the best interest of a minor," Eric explained. "I will petition the court for an order for Becca to act as Kelly's GAL and accompany her to all her classes for a few days. Of course, the school officials will know who she is. However, since she looks young enough, she's going to pose as a student so she can observe the behavior and actions of the students who are harassing Kelly. If we think we have just cause, then we'll file a lawsuit against the parents. This may take time."

Mrs. Richards appeared confused. "She'll accompany her to all her classes?" She turned to look at Kelly.

"Yes," Eric said. "I'll file the petition today. We should have the order tomorrow. Until then, Kelly doesn't have to go to school until Becca goes with her."

Kelly turned towards Becca as she continued to wipe the tears from her eyes.

Eric continued. "Becca will go over all the details with you, Kelly." He stood. "Please go with her to the conference room. Your mother and I need to go over some legal issues."

They stood and left the office. Kelly followed Becca to the other conference room.

———◆———

Mrs. Richards looked at Eric across the table. "Tell me more about this Guardian ad Litem."

"This will be the best way for Becca to infiltrate the school and pass herself off as a student and Kelly's friend."

"What if the other students suspect that she's a court appointed…"

Eric answered, "GAL."

"Yes. Then they will be on their best behavior," said Mrs. Richards.

"It's a chance we have to take. Let's hope the students believe she's one of them. Becca has a strong personality. I trust she'll get to the bottom of your daughter's bullying."

"Yes, I like what she told Kelly about the song. I think it gave her some comfort. I didn't want to say anything while Kelly was here, but I'm so upset with those kids who are making her react this way. They were texting her and posting bad things about her on social media. I took her phone today so she wouldn't have to see it all." She took the phone out and handed it to Eric. "I even monitor her computer. I allow her to use it strictly for homework. It's exhausting, but I don't want her to read all that cyber garbage. I haven't erased anything. I'm saving it for proof. I know I told you that I want to sue them. Do you think it's possible to sue their parents? I want someone to take responsibility for my child's misery." Mrs. Richards had a sob in her voice. She put her head in her hands.

Eric looked at the phone and read some of the horrendous text messages. He shook his head. "I'm sorry Kelly had to be a victim of this harassment. I promise we'll catch those who are bullying her. Are you willing to wait?"

"I'll wait until the end of time as long as I have my sweet, passionate girl back." Her voice cracked again.

"I think that's possible. When I think it's necessary, I'll ask you to bring in her cell phone and computer. I'll use them for evidence."

Mrs. Richards sat up straight in her chair. "Where do I sign, and how much do you want to get things going? I don't care what the cost, I only want my daughter to get justice and become whole again."

This time, Eric knew both he and Becca were going to earn the fee.

CHAPTER 11

BECCA LED KELLY TO THE small conference room. Again, eyes followed as they walked. She had to do this on her own and didn't want to let Eric down. He had full confidence in her.

Kelly resumed her stone face while Becca pointed to a seat. "Sit here, Kelly; it has a lovely view of the garden outdoors." Kelly glanced out the window and then lowered her eyes.

Becca took a breath and tried not to appear nervous. "What type of surgeon do you want to be?"

Kelly squinted and looked at Becca but didn't answer.

"Have you decided yet?"

Kelly spoke softly. "I think I want to be a heart surgeon."

"I admire you. That's a very noble profession."

Eyes down, Kelly slowly nodded her head in agreement as if thinking about her decision. Becca thought Kelly might be realizing this herself for the first time.

"As we discussed in Mr. Jefferies' office, the court will allow me to be your GAL, a companion in your classes. I'm going to observe the students, see their behavior towards you and each other…I want to see what's going on. And I want everyone to know that we're friends. The teachers will know who I am, but we want the other students to think I'm a student too. Do you think we can pull that off?"

While Becca was talking, Kelly's facial expression changed. Her eyes widened and she opened her mouth as if to speak.

Becca could tell she never expected this.

Then Kelly spoke softly. "Will we sit together at lunch?"

"Of course, that's the idea…to show everyone that we're friends. Even if you have any close friends, you can't tell them what we're doing. This must come across as natural."

Kelly kept blinking her eyes as though she was awakening from a deep sleep. "I really don't have any close friends."

Becca didn't think she had. *The poor kid.*

"We're going to change all that. I promise things will be better. The kids that are—" Becca hesitated, trying to avoid the word 'bullying.' "—giving you a problem had a choice. They could have joined the crowd or, unfortunately, become a victim. That's what happened to you, Kelly. You didn't want to join them, so they made you a target."

Becca noticed Kelly withdrew and seemed to have her stone face back again. She knew this was a challenge for both of them.

Can she still be having thoughts of suicide? I hope I can help this sweet, frail girl who was once an A student. Has she fallen into an abyss so deep that she can never recover?

"I want you to know that we're all on your side. We'll do our best to turn this unfortunate incident around. You know, Kelly, I'm going to need your help."

Kelly tilted her head again. Becca realized this was her way of asking "what" without saying anything.

"Yes, I'm going to need your help with my outfits and hairstyle. I see you're wearing a ponytail. I'm going to wear my hair in a ponytail too."

Kelly kept looking at Becca, but still didn't say a word.

Jason told her to tell Kelly about her braces. She didn't know if she should tell her now or wait for another time. She decided to tell her now. Becca wanted Kelly to know that she was not immune to bullying. She relayed the story. While she described how the kids called her "wired," Kelly listened intently. Becca looked Kelly in the eye as Jason had suggested.

"It's terrible when kids call you names." Becca tried to win her confidence.

Kelly only nodded.

"I'm glad I listened to my dad. Now I can smile a lot."

Kelly kept nodding. At least she wasn't looking down. She was staring at Becca's teeth. Then she spoke in a low voice causing Becca to lean towards her to hear.

"I'm afraid to go back to school. They scared me yesterday. They don't want me around." Then she lowered her head, put her hand to her face, and cried softly. "They hate me."

"They don't hate you, Kelly; they hate themselves."

Kelly removed her hand from her face, turned to Becca, and tilted her head. She didn't understand that statement.

Becca stood and put her hand lightly on Kelly's shoulder. "Trust me, when this is all over you'll realize that they really hate themselves. You don't have to go back until I'm there with you. We're going to take care of this problem. I promise you."

Becca had a stabbing pain in her heart thinking about what was said to Kelly to make her feel this frightened. She was determined to get to the bottom of it and help her become whole again.

Just then, there was a knock on the door. It was Eric and Mrs. Richards.

Mrs. Richards gave Kelly a hug. "It's going to be okay, sweetheart."

Kelly looked confused. Her heart wanted all this to go away, but her brain was reluctant.

"It should take a day or two to get a court order for Becca to be your GAL. Is there anything you want to ask us before you leave?"

Kelly took a deep breath, let out a sigh, and spoke softly, "Can I really be a doctor?"

Mrs. Richards and Eric looked at each other. Eric spoke, "Definitely. And I want to be your first patient."

Kelly smiled through tear-stained eyes.

———◆———

After Kelly and Mrs. Richards left, Eric asked Becca to join him in his office. He closed the door and told her to sit.

Becca took a breath. "This is a serious case. Do you think your plan for me to infiltrate the kids will work?"

"I don't know, but it's worth a shot. That is…if you still want to do it? I want an affirmative answer from you. You met with Kelly. What do you think?"

"After meeting Kelly, I want to more than ever."

"You have a lot on your plate. You're going to school, and you have a job here. You'll have to come here every day after school and make a report. Are you up to this?"

Becca looked at Eric, shook her head, and spoke slowly, "Yes…I want to give it a try. If I don't, I'll regret it for the rest of my life."

"Okay, I'll set the wheels in motion for the order."

———◆———

It was almost five o'clock. After Kelly and Mrs. Richards left the office, Becca researched all she could about being a Guardian ad Litem. She realized this was the only way to catch the offending students red-handed. When she attended high school, six years ago, cell phones were not used as they are today. With the touch of a finger, all sorts of horrible statements go out instantly to many over the internet. Today cyberbullying is a cause of suicides. Becca wanted to be able to help stop a possible suicide.

Now, she had to tell her mother and father just what she was doing. She knew she had to do a lot of convincing. After all, she was the only child of caring parents.

As USUAL, THE AROMA OF something delicious wafted throughout the house. After greeting her parents, Becca went to her room to freshen up before dinner. She was tired from a busy day at the office. She changed out of work clothes into something more comfortable.

"Hey, Mom, do you want me to set the table yet?" she asked as she walked into the kitchen. It was her favorite room in the house. Ever since she was young, she and her parents had wonderful conversations there. There was a small round table for four in a nook in the room where most of their meals took place. Since there were only the three of them, they rarely ate in the formal dining room, which was used for guests and festivities.

"Thanks, dear. Dinner's almost ready."

Becca started to set the table. "Where's Pops?

"He's in his den finishing up some paper work. How was your day?"

If her mother didn't ask that same question every day, Becca would flip out. She was ready with all the stories of the day. She started to tell her about the elderly gentleman who was erroneously charged with the case of road rage. As she was talking, her father walked into the room.

"Wait, wait, I want to hear this. There's so much of that going around. People are crazy these days. They pull out guns in some cases of road rage."

"Hi, Dad," she said as she gave her father a peck on the cheek.

"Well, this didn't include a gun. However, the crazy guy caused the elderly man to run into him. I'm so happy we have an eyewitness coming in to dispute the other man's argument that it was reckless driving on the old guy's part."

"Good for the eyewitness." Her father smiled and gave her a hug. "Sounds like you and your office are doing a fine job."

"There's something else I wanted to discuss with the both of you. I thought I'd tell you after dinner."

Both parents looked at her, then at each other. "Well, when you put it that way," her father said, glancing again at her mother, "we want to hear it now."

Her mother nodded.

"Okay. We have a new case of school bullying. Eric is petitioning the court for an order for me to be a Guardian ad Litem to help our new client whose daughter is threatening to kill herself."

Her father interrupted. "Guardian ad Litem? Isn't that for children of families that are in crises? Doesn't a guardian observe the family and make recommendations for the children? Or even place them in foster care?"

"Yes, Dad. But in this case, Eric will write the petition to read that I will accompany Kelly to her classes to observe any bullying towards her. I will then report to the court. We're hoping that after my submission, we can sue the parents of the offending children. Eric thinks I can get to the source of the bullying. Because I still look young enough, he wanted me to act as a student and try to gain confidence."

Her parents were quiet for a few seconds. Then her father spoke. "Don't they have young-looking police women for that job?" Before she could answer he said, "Will there be any danger on your part?"

"I don't think so. All of the school officials will know I'm her GAL. I'll also be working closely with Officer Regino of the local police department. He came in today to tell us of another case that ended, sadly, in suicide."

"I don't know if I like this, Becca." Her mother's eyebrows knitted in a worried look.

"Don't worry, Mom, I know the ropes. I saw some cases of bullying when I was in school. Some guys and girls are vulnerable, and they're the ones the bullies target."

"I don't know…" Her mother looked uncertain.

"Marion, our daughter has a good head on her shoulders. If she can help with this problem, she'll be saving someone's life."

"Yes," Becca agreed. "And since the school officials know who I am, I'll be totally protected. I really want to help."

"Will they have an undercover police officer as well?"

"I don't know, Dad. I'll find out when we talk to Officer Regino."

"What if they start bullying *you*?" her father asked.

"That's the idea. I want to see who the students are so I can let the police know."

"I have to say, Becca, it really worries me."

"I'll be alright. Remember, you two, I'm on eagle's wings."

Her father smiled and shook his head. "Sometimes I regret telling you that. It makes you think you're Supergirl."

"Even so, how can we be sure?" asked her mother. "Let's discuss it further at dinner."

While they were eating, Becca tried to convince her parents that she was safe and knew what she was doing. The more she talked, the more she convinced even herself. She knew this was something she wanted to do, and she would be involved in knowing who was bullying Kelly.

One of the reasons Becca wanted to become an attorney was to help people. She was passionate about this. Both she and Eric were on the same page when it came to helping clients.

While she was getting ready for bed, she thought of the elder Mr. Jefferies and how much she had learned from him. It was his encouragement that led to her decision to go back to school and study law. She was grateful that Eric took his place in the firm, and that she was allowed to work with him as she did with his father.

She thought of Kelly and how upset and frightened she was. *I have to change that. I have to gain her confidence.* After Kelly and her mother left the office, Eric shared some of the texts and Facebook posts sent out over the internet pertaining to Kelly. It was extremely hurtful. They accused her of being a slut, a fat pig who slept with everyone in the tenth grade. She had hundreds of texts from guys and girls propositioning her. The incident in the cafeteria the day before frightened her so much that she refused to go back to school. Her mother even told her that she would try to enroll her in another school. Kelly refused, telling her mother it would be the same wherever she went.

Becca felt a grave responsibility to help. Being her GAL would give Kelly the courage to go back to school. *I have to convince her that I will be there to help her and not let any harm come to her. Can I pull it off?* Becca was truly fearless. Her father knew it as well as her mother, and probably the elder Mr. Jefferies. Becca fell asleep dreaming of all the possibilities of what could happen when she went back to high school with Kelly.

CHAPTER 13

BECCA HAD A FULL MORNING and couldn't believe it was after twelve. She had rushed out of the house, forgetting to pack herself a lunch. She thought of going to the deli that Eric introduced her to. She loved their tuna. She glanced at her phone, which was blinking, indicating she had voice mail. It was Jason Regino wishing her luck with the case. She was about to erase it and hang up when she heard him say, "If you're not busy for lunch, maybe we could meet to discuss some issues. I know I can help."

Becca sat there holding the phone, the automated voice was saying, "press seven to delete, press nine to save." Becca didn't know why, but she pressed nine.

Jason had given her his number yesterday. She punched in the number not knowing what she would say.

"Officer Regino," Jason answered.

"Hi Jason, this is Becca at the lawyers' office. I got your message. I was thinking of going to a local deli to pick up a tuna sandwich. If you like, you can join me there."

"That's great. I'm still on my lunch break and I'm close to your office. Tell me where it is, and I'll meet you."

Becca told him, and when she hung up, she had a smile on her face. She grabbed her purse and headed out.

It was a short walk, and she got there within ten minutes. She found a table and sat. After a few minutes, the waitress came over to take her order. Jason wasn't there yet. "I'm waiting for someone; he should be here shortly."

Just as she said that, Jason walked over to the table. "Did you order yet?"

"No, but now that you're here we can both order. How did you get here so fast?"

"I told you I was close by."

The waitress had a sassy smile on her face. "Hello, Officer; that was good timing. What can I get you both?"

Becca ordered her tuna and a cup of hot green tea.

"That sounds good," said Jason, "all except that hot green tea. I'll have an iced tea."

The waitress took their order, raised an eyebrow at Becca as if to say, "You go girl," and walked away.

Becca tried not to blush. She could only imagine what the waitress was thinking.

Jason started to talk. "I'm glad you're going in as a GAL. I think you'll be able to help the situation. How'd it go with the girl?"

"She's really frightened. She's being bullied big time. I learned about some of the texts and Facebook postings. They were bad."

"Yeah, I know. Kids can be cruel." Jason spoke with authority. Becca thought it funny because he was so young himself. He continued. "Yesterday you thought I knew a lot about the subject. I do because *I* was bullied in high school."

"*You*...I find that hard to believe." Becca scrunched her eyebrows.

"I know. I was different in high school. I was scrawny and shy, a perfect target. My mother found a terrible message scribbled on one of my books. She told my father. They were irate. I begged them not to go to the principal because I knew what the kids would do to me. My dad always liked going to the gym and thought this was a perfect time for me to go with him. Before, when he would ask me to join him, I always made excuses."

Becca put her elbow on the table and her hand to her cheek. She was amazed at what Jason was saying.

"Now that I think of it, I *was* sort of a nerd. I went to the gym with him, and before you knew it, instead of scrawny, I bulked up. The guys on the football team became interested in me. They bugged me to try out. I did and became a tackle. I want to tell you, that let out all my frustrations. Believe me; the kids didn't bully me anymore."

"That's fascinating, Jason. Looking at you now, it's hard to believe." Becca still had her hand to her cheek. The waitress came over with their drinks. She had a wide grin on her face. Embarrassed, Becca put her hand down in her lap.

"Your sandwiches are coming." The waitress winked at Becca.

"Good, we don't have much time. We both have to get back to work," said Becca trying not to blush again. To no avail, her face felt hot.

Jason talked a little more about his experiences. Becca asked many questions, and he was all too happy to respond. When the waitress brought their sandwiches, they were deep in conversation and practically ignored her. When Becca glanced up to say thank you, she was nodding her head in approval. Obviously, she thought Jason was a good catch. In her subconscious, so did Becca.

———◆———

Back at the office, Becca couldn't stop thinking of Jason. He was so polite, and not bad to look at. He explained to her that the weak, shy, scrawny, and obese were targets for bullies. When he joined the football team, they stopped picking on him. All he had to do was give one of them a look, and they walked in the opposite direction. He told her that after his experience, he was an advocate for the victims of bullying. Whenever he saw any of the students being targeted, he always came to their defense and helped in any way he could. That's why he is passionate about the subject. And that's why he became a police officer.

His personality goes so deep; it's like peeling an onion. I thought Eric had many layers.

Eric came out of his office and, as was his habit, knocked on her cubicle. "I got some news for you. Judge Andrews just signed the order. We'll get it this afternoon. You're officially Kelly's GAL. We can call Mrs. Richards and tell her you'll pick Kelly up tomorrow. Do you want me to go with you?"

"That would be great. Will you call the principal for an appointment to introduce us?"

"Yes, I can take care of that. I want you to read the petition. Familiarize yourself with it. It describes why and what you'll be doing as Kelly's GAL. I had to be very creative."

"I believe you. I'm familiar with your petitions."

"By the way, do you have school tonight?"

"Yes." Becca shook her head and started to think, *how can I do all this?*

As though reading her mind, Eric said, "Don't come in until ten tomorrow. You can sleep in."

"What about Kelly. She'll miss her first period class."

"It's okay. She's missed so much already. It's important you be with her."

"But I have so much work to do. I don't only have this case."

"You do now. I assigned all your other work to Carolyn. She was more than willing to help. You have some friends around here, Curtis."

Becca was stunned. In the back of her mind, she didn't know how she was going to handle the caseload. All she knew was that she wanted to help Kelly. Now a weight was lifted off her shoulders, and she could concentrate on law school and high school—and of course—Kelly. Eric wanted her full attention on this case.

Becca was staring at Eric in awe. *How kind and considerate he is.* She was at a loss for words.

"Okay, I'll be here at ten ready to go back to high school."

"Remember to make sure you dress the part. You have to be convincing as a high school student, and one that is vulnerable."

Becca's eyes widened. "Oh Eric, I forgot about that. I need to look the part of someone who is ripe for the picking."

"You don't want to overdo it. Just act shy and vulnerable. I'm going to call Mrs. Richards this afternoon to tell her that we'll pick Kelly up between ten-thirty and ten forty-five."

Becca thought about her own parents. Last night she had to convince them that she was ready, willing, and able to do this. Now she had to convince herself.

CHAPTER 14

—◆—

BECCA WOKE LATE. SHE WAS happy Eric told her to sleep in. While she was getting dressed, she remembered her discussion with her parents at dinner about going to school as Kelly's GAL. Her mother was upset, as she knew she would be. When her mother asked if a police officer would be a better choice, Becca told her that a GAL would be more advantageous to the client. What upset her most was her father's attitude. After their discussion, he just stared at her without blinking. She kept quiet while her mother complained, and when she was finished, he stood, kissed Becca on the cheek, patted her back, and left the room. His silence was deafening. Becca knew him well. Even though he told her mother it would be fine, Becca knew he was not happy about the GAL appointment, but he respected his daughter's decision. Now it was up to her to prove that everything would be all right. *Oh God, help me out with this. Place me in the palm of your hand.*

She finished dressing in blue jeans, a casual shirt, and sneakers. Wanting to look the part of a high school senior, she remembered to put her long blonde hair in a ponytail. She wore very little makeup, just a light blush. Glancing in the mirror, she was surprised that the ponytail did the trick. Kelly would be happy when she saw her. Becca ate a quick breakfast and left for work.

When she walked into the office at ten a.m., everyone commented on her looks and teased her about keeping bankers' hours.

Eric's door was open. She peeked in, and he waved her inside. "Look at you, Miss Teenager. Are you ready to go?"

"Yes, if you are. Do you want to go over some last minute details?"

"No, but you can give Carolyn a heads up on the scope of your work and what she can do for you while you're gone. I don't want our other cases neglected. Be ready to go in fifteen minutes."

Becca went to her desk, pulled some files, and went to see Carolyn whose cubicle was on the other side of the office. On the way there, she ran into Luke Hawkins, the office flirt. He let out a loud whistle. Becca's face flushed in embarrassment. *He knows what's going on. Why is he such a... I'm going to have to find out what a high school kid would say in this case. Probably some choice four-letter words.*

When she passed him, he whistled again. "Hello, cutie."

What a jerk. I don't have time for this right now. "Good morning, Luke. Wish I could return the sentiment." She always gave him a hard time.

Carolyn was very nice. She greeted Becca, took the files, spoke about the work a few minutes, and wished her luck. She got back to Eric's office within the fifteen minutes. "I'm ready to go."

"Okay, give me a minute. I'll be right out."

Eric was doing a wonderful job covering all his father's cases. Now he had this very serious one. Becca knew that he couldn't devote all his time to this case, and he was relying on her to cover her end. She was going to do her best to make him proud.

While they were driving to pick up Kelly, Eric told her not to worry, that she certainly looked the part, and that he would get any information that she needed to make this case a success.

"It's going to be difficult. Even though it's only a few years, you're going to have to learn a new way of communicating."

Becca was most worried about this, and she told Eric.

"Here's what you do. Listen. Don't be the first to open your mouth. Say hello and let them do all the talking. Pay attention to their hand gestures and their vocabulary. Try to get the knack of it before you carry on a conversation. If you do this, you won't have a problem."

"What if some catch on and realize I'm Kelly's GAL?"

"Just be honest. Tell them you're there to observe her classes. I'm hoping this won't be the case. You look authentic. I believe they'll think you're a student."

———◆———

They picked Kelly up at ten forty-five. She took one look at Becca and blinked several times.

"Hello, Kelly, do you approve?" Kelly could only nod. She looked better than yesterday. At least her outfit didn't have wrinkles.

Arriving at Mrs. Franklin's office, they waited because the appointment was last minute. She already had an eleven o'clock appointment and would be free at eleven thirty.

In her mid-fifties, the principal had graying brown hair that gave her the appearance of being older. She was short and thin and dressed impeccably in a royal blue blouse, off-white skirt, and a necklace the same color as her skirt. Her shoes were the same color as her blouse. Looking at her, one knew she was a person of detail. Becca thought she probably had a wardrobe of shoes to match every outfit.

Mrs. Franklin asked Kelly to wait in the reception area while she spoke to Eric and Becca. There was a window in the office that allowed Kelly to view them. Becca knew Kelly would feel safe as long as she could see them.

"Please sit, Mr. Jefferies, Miss Curtis." Mrs. Franklin knew about the bullying and received the petition and order via email that morning.

"Mrs. Franklin, it was so kind of you to meet with us. It's very important to our case that Becca remains close to Kelly, observing her and the students she comes in contact with. Becca will be an eyewitness, corroborating the bullying."

"And what do you think you'll gain with this information?" the principal asked sternly.

"We want to find out who is tormenting Kelly and put a stop to it."

"I assume she *is* going to counseling, isn't she? Can't that person determine this?"

"It's very difficult. She's not opening up. Her mother is very worried that she'll become so withdrawn and possibly try to...." He dropped off and didn't want to say suicide.

"Yes, yes, I know. There are horrible things going on. The children of the cyber generation are extremely trying. This is the reason I'm agreeing to this project. I want to get to the bottom of it as well. We have zero tolerance for bullying in this school. When you find out, we will suspend whomever immediately."

Becca sat there as an observer. She was brought back to her own high school days. Being there, walking through the halls, seeing the teenagers, her emotions were a mix of elation and fear. Elated to go back in time, but fearful that she might be exposed, she had to remember what Eric told her. It was going to be difficult for her. Because she was usually an outspoken individual, she now had to adjust her personality to listening. Her main objective was to find out who was bullying Kelly, and making her so afraid.

"Now, Miss Curtis…Becca, correct?"

Becca nodded. Remembering what Eric said, she listened.

"I have written a letter of introduction for you to give to all the teachers. You can show it before the class begins. Kelly's lunch period starts in thirty minutes. You and Kelly should go directly there. She knows where it is. After lunch, you'll accompany Kelly to her afternoon classes."

Mrs. Franklin turned toward Eric. "I would never have approved of *any* of this without a court order. We do have police officers stationed throughout the school. However, the children are very sneaky in their attempts at bullying. One of the high schools just recently had a suicide due to bullying. So far, we've had none. I wish to keep it that way. I must admit, this seems to be the only way to get to the bottom of the situation." Then she addressed Becca. "You'll be reporting to Mr. Jefferies, and he'll be reporting to me. Good luck, and I say wholeheartedly, God be with you."

—◆—

CHAPTER 15

AFTER SPEAKING WITH THE PRINCIPAL, Eric and Becca returned to the reception area where Kelly waited. Eric patted both girls on the shoulder. "I'll be back at three. Meet me in the parking lot." He looked from Kelly to Becca. "Good luck." He left to go back to the office.

Becca smiled at Kelly. "I guess we go to lunch together. It's a little early, so we'll wait for the bell. Is there anything you want to go over with me?"

Kelly was sighing and wringing her hands. Becca knew she didn't want to be there.

"Listen, Kelly, I know how you feel. But this is the only way to stop the kids from bothering you. We're going to resolve this once and for all. I will be with you every minute."

Becca felt Kelly's trembling hand touch hers. "I'm afraid to go to the cafeteria," she said.

"I know," Becca said. "I know." At the office meeting, Mrs. Richards told Becca and Eric the details of

Kelly's ordeal on Monday. Today was Thursday and she hadn't been back since.

The lunch bell rang. Becca had a lump in her throat. *It's show time.* She had to tell herself everything was going to be fine, and all of this was for Kelly, who needed to be whole again.

They walked through the halls to the cafeteria. It all started coming back to Becca. There it was, as though she had never left. The room was noisy. Students laughing, some were singing. Boys flirted with girls, and the response was, "Get lost." Papers from straws were flying around. She began to relax. *Not too much has changed.* The room was crowded making it almost impossible to find a table.

"Let's get our lunch first. Do you know what you want to eat?" said Becca.

Kelly shrugged and walked to the food line.

Becca got her regular tuna, and so did Kelly. "Where do you want to sit?" she asked Kelly, who motioned to a remote table in the back.

A few of the nearby boys were pointing at her and shouting something Becca couldn't hear. As they walked to the table, Kelly grabbed Becca's arm and froze. "It's them, it's them. I'm scared."

Becca looked around to see to whom she was referring. "Don't worry, Kelly. I won't let anything happen to you."

They sat at the table and began to eat their lunch. Becca's cell phone vibrated. She took it out of her purse to read the text. It was Eric wishing her good luck. She texted back, "thanks," and left the phone on the table.

Two of the boys who had been shouting came over. "What's a cute girl like you sitting with frog face?" said one of them while the other laughed and pointed at Kelly. Becca thought they might be Kelly's bullies.

Sitting next to Kelly, Becca could feel her body tighten. It took all of Becca's restraint to say nothing, remembering Eric's advice. She wanted to tell the pimple-faced jerk who was laughing to shut up. Instead, she just looked at him with squinted eyes, then turned towards Kelly. "Yum, the tuna's good."

"They have delicious tuna. I like it too," Kelly said in a monotonous tone.

"Hey, get the blimp more food. That's not enough to fill her up," said the pimply-faced boy.

Becca held her tongue. *Quiet, quiet, keep your mouth shut.* Now she was raging inside, but she kept her cool. After a long, uncomfortable stare she couldn't help herself and said, "Besides Pimple Face, what do they call you?"

"Ooh, she talks. My name is Ryan, what's your name? You new here?"

Becca was pleased he thought she was a student. She raised her eyebrow and didn't answer him. Instead, she turned toward Kelly. "Thanks for suggesting the tuna. It's great."

Kelly looked at Becca and tilted her head in confusion. Becca actually picked the tuna first.

The two boys went to a different table and started picking on another boy who looked timid and shy.

Becca whispered to Kelly, "Do you know them? What are their names?"

Kelly nodded.

"Quickly, tell me," said Becca.

Kelly whispered, "The one with the bad complexion is Ryan Hall, and the other is Ethan Weeks. The kid they're teasing now is Michael James. They're all in my biology class."

Becca watched as Ryan glanced around the room, seemingly to make sure none of the teachers or police officers were looking. Then he threw Michael's lunch on the floor. When Michael bent down to pick it up, Ethan kicked him. They both walked away laughing, calling him names. Michael's face flushed, and he seemed to be cursing under his breath.

Becca felt sorry for him. Her first instinct was to get up and help Michael, but had to restrain herself.

Kelly made a whimpering sound at the sight of the two boys harassing Michael. Becca rubbed Kelly's back and whispered in her ear, "Eagle's wings."

Somehow, that phrase seemed to calm her. She gave Becca a faint smile.

"I'm here for you, Kelly."

As Becca was consoling Kelly, Ryan, Ethan, and two other boys came back to the table. They sat down surrounding the girls, two on each side.

Kelly stiffened again and moved closer to Becca.

One of the boys, who appeared to be the ring-leader, sat next to Becca. She kept eating her lunch as though he weren't there.

"Are you a senior, sexy girl?" he said putting his face close to Becca's.

Becca didn't say a word; her eyes met his and locked for several seconds.

He moved his head closer, grabbed her arm and said, "I'm talkin' to you, bitch."

By now, Becca was fuming. She shucked her arm loose and wanted to rattle off some nasty expletives but kept calm and continued eating her sandwich. Meanwhile, Ryan was on the other side of Kelly, giving her a hard time.

Becca turned to Ryan. "Back off, Pimple Face." It came out without thought. Becca was instinctively protecting Kelly.

Three of the boys started talking and laughing at once.

"Woo woo."

"Little frog face has a friend."

"Did you hear that, Dylan?" Ryan said to the ring-leader. "She talks."

Dylan, still sitting next to Becca, said in a low growling voice, "You don't know who you're messing with, girl."

Now Becca had enough, she couldn't hold back any longer. She narrowed her eyes and responded in her angriest voice. "Just *who* am I messing with?"

Tony Sorvino said, "She's rad, Dylan, I'll bet she's great in the sack." He stood up and gyrated.

Several girls from a nearby table started to laugh and call out, "Lookin' good, Tony. Don't waste your time on those losers." More laughter.

Dylan spotted Becca's phone on the table. He snatched it and started typing numbers into it. She tried to get it away from him, but he quickly turned his back and continued typing. He then threw it on the table. She grabbed it and put it in her purse. Dylan turned to Becca and spoke in a low menacing voice that sent chills through her body. "I'm not through with you. You better watch your back, if you know what's good for you. I wouldn't want anything to happen to that pretty face of yours."

She didn't like the fact that he was threatening her. Unable to keep quiet, her anger got the best of her. "Oh yeah, tough guy, why don't you go play with your stooges"—she jerked her thumb at Ryan and Tony—"and leave us alone?"

He gave Becca an intimidating glare, got up, and left the table. The other three followed laughing.

When they left, Becca turned to Kelly and noticed her hand shaking when she picked up her glass. "Are you okay? Don't worry. I'm going to fix this. That's why I'm here. Please trust me."

Kelly couldn't talk. She had tears in her eyes and lay her head down on the table.

"I'll take care of those boys. Leave it to me. I want you to concentrate on your classes and your school-work. When those bullies talk to you, don't pay attention. Try to think of your career and how much you want to be a surgeon."

Kelly lifted her head and turned toward Becca. She gave her a faint smile while a tear trickled down her cheek.

"That a girl. I heard them call the other two boys Dylan and Tony. Do you know them?"

"Yes. They're in my English class, Dylan Baker and Tony Sorvino."

Becca patted Kelly's hand and wrote the names on her pad. "Great. I think English is next?"

Kelly nodded.

The lunch bell rang and Becca stood. "Okay, on to your next class."

Again, Kelly nodded. Becca realized it was an effort for her to speak.

"Good. Let's go. Remember, school, studies, and nothing else. Leave all the bad stuff to me. I promise you, I'll take care of it."

Becca was so concerned with Kelly's welfare that she forgot to check her phone to see what Dylan had done to it.

CHAPTER 16

— ✦ —

WHEN THEY WALKED INTO THE classroom, it was noisy. Students talked, laughed, and used profanity. Before the bell rang, Becca took the principal's letter to Mrs. Farmer, the English teacher. Mrs. Franklin indicated in the letter that Becca was there as Kelly's Guardian ad Litem. However, the teacher should be discreet and not divulge this to the students. Becca was there to observe and not participate in the class. The bell rang and the students settled down.

She and Kelly found two seats in the back. Becca's eyes roamed around the room. She spotted Dylan with Tony. Because they were talking to some of the girls, they didn't see her.

The class settled down when Mrs. Farmer spoke. "Okay, we're going to continue our discussion of *Hamlet.*"

Becca was a good student and loved the story of *Hamlet. Good, something familiar.*

Dylan sat in the middle of the classroom with Tony next to him. Becca noticed him looking around the room until he spotted her and Kelly. She inwardly flinched when he glared at her, narrowing his eyes and shaking his head. Becca thought he was evil and menacing. *Poor Kelly. Imagine being bullied by him. He almost scares me.*

Tony stood and said, "To be or not to be. Is that the question?" Everyone laughed.

"Sit down, Mr. Sorvino," said Mrs. Farmer, "you'll have your turn to recite."

Becca wrote *Tony Sorvino* on her note pad. Next to his name, she wrote *gyrator*. She jotted Dylan's name and next to it wrote *terminator*. Later, at the office, she would type it into her official notes.

Tony spoke again. "I did my homework, Mrs. Farmer."

Someone from the back oinked like a pig.

"That will be enough. I allow you to be creative in this class, but I will *not* tolerate insults. The next time I hear that, I'm going to send someone to the principal's office," Mrs. Farmer said in a stern voice as she picked up a book from her desk. "We're going over Hamlet's soliloquy. Take out your books."

A boy in the back started rapping a few of the lines. "To be…or not… to be…that is…the question."

"Okay, Joseph, since you insist on giving us a recitation, why don't you come to the front and let everyone hear it?"

"Nah, nah," said Joseph, "I just rap it out. That's how I remember the words."

"Well then, come up front and rap for us." Mrs. Farmer was serious. She gave the students every opportunity to learn. By this time, everyone was cheering him on.

Joseph went to the front of the room and began to rap the rest of the soliloquy. Though he changed some of the words, he got most of it right. It was remarkable. Becca thought it was a great way to remember the lines. When he finished, he took a bow. Everyone clapped and shouted.

"Settle down, settle down," Mrs. Farmer said with a wide grin on her face.

"That was very good, Joseph. Now can you tell me what all that means?"

"Nah, I just rap the words, I don't know what they mean."

"It's wonderful that you can do that, but your assignment was to decipher the meaning."

Mrs. Farmer asked a few other students to interpret the first few lines. Becca became interested. It had been a few years since she'd read *Hamlet*. Suddenly her cell phone vibrated in her purse. She took it out. There was a text from an unknown number.

Be careful bitch. Watch your back.
I'll be waiting for you outside.

Becca looked straight at Dylan. He was glaring at her. He lifted his finger to his neck and slid it across his throat from ear to ear. Becca glanced at Kelly to see if she saw Dylan's gesture. She was relieved Kelly hadn't seen it; her eyes were on her book. Even though it was disturbing, Becca tried to appear calm.

Inside she was shaking.

When she accepted this assignment, she never thought she would encounter something as frightening as this. In one short hour, she'd become a target. She couldn't wait to tell Jason and Eric. She was there to help Kelly, but now she needed to protect *herself.*

Mrs. Farmer called Kelly's name. "What are your thoughts?"

Kelly looked up from her book but didn't respond.

One of the girls shouted, "Hey, frog girl, she's talking to you."

Becca blinked and tapped Kelly's shoulder.

Mrs. Farmer gave the girl a stern look of rebuke and turned her attention to Kelly. "Can you please read from '*to die to sleep no more*' down to '*there's the respect that makes calamity of so long life,*' and tell us what you think that means?"

Earlier the principal was talking about kids committing suicide, and here the lesson is about Hamlet contemplating just that. Now, a boy she met, briefly, was threatening her. Becca's head was spinning.

Kelly spoke in a low voice. "He was talking about dying."

"Yes, that's correct, can you tell us more?"

Kelly pursed her lips and shook her head. Becca knew Kelly was having her own thoughts of suicide, and talking about it in class would be painful.

Some of the students were mocking her. Telling her to "get with it, we don't play in this room."

Dylan kept looking at Becca, and the expression on his face was demonic. It gave her shivers down her spine. *Why did I sign up for this? Am I crazy?* She was glad Kelly didn't see his glare. She was listening to the teacher.

The lesson went on with Dylan occasionally turning to look at Becca. At one point, Becca saw Kelly look over at Dylan. Her body visibly tightened. She turned and glanced at Becca.

Becca shook her head, putting on a brave face to let Kelly know there was nothing to worry about. But deep down *she* was scared.

The bell rang. The kids scrambled out of the room laughing and yelling at each other while quoting Shakespeare.

Becca was reluctant to walk out of the classroom knowing that Dylan would be waiting. She was trying to think of a plan to divert him. As luck would have it, when they walked out of the room, a police officer was stationed outside next to Mrs. Farmer's classroom. Becca couldn't believe her eyes.

Dylan Baker waited outside. He stood opposite the police officer as he watched the two walk past him. Becca locked eyes with him for one second. His face contorted. He narrowed his eyes and clenched his fists. He mouthed something she could only imagine that indicated he was angry to see the police officer.

At that moment, another coincidence happened. Mrs. Franklin walked past them in the opposite direction. She went into Mrs. Farmer's classroom.

Becca slowed her pace, waited for Dylan to leave, and told Kelly to wait next to the police officer, then doubled back to the classroom. The principal was talking to Mrs. Farmer. She politely interrupted and showed Mrs. Franklin the text.

"Who wrote this? This is immediate cause for suspension. I will not tolerate such threatening." Becca told her about the cell phone incident in the lunchroom.

"If you dial the number," said Becca, "I'll bet you get Dylan Baker."

Mrs. Farmer said, "You have to watch out for Dylan. He seems to be some sort of a leader, and is an angry young man."

"I know Dylan," said Mrs. Franklin. "He has paid many visits to my office. He's been accused of harming other students. However, there has never been proof. His home life is bad, and he takes it out on other kids. He's violent and has been in several fights."

"Don't worry, Mrs. Franklin. When I find out who text this, and I think it's him, I'll have proof," said Becca.

"I'll make sure all his teachers observe his behavior while you're here," said Mrs. Franklin. "We don't want anything happening to our students, and especially their Guardian ad-Litems. Let me know if there are any other incidents."

Becca agreed she would and hurried back to Kelly, who was still standing next to the police officer.

"Okay, let's go to your next class."

CHAPTER 17

MATH WAS NOT ONE OF Becca's favorite subjects, especially algebra. When they walked into the classroom, she noticed the students talking in a quiet tone. They were not as boisterous as those in the English class. While she searched for a seat, she asked Kelly if Dylan or any of the others were in this class. When Kelly told her they were not, and she gave a silent sigh of relief. Becca took the letter to Mrs. Gilroy. As in the previous class, the teacher nodded and told her to take a seat.

The bell rang, and the first boy Mrs. Gilroy called on was Michael James, who sat a few rows from her. He seemed to be a good student and knew all the answers. A few times, she noticed that Michael turned and glanced at her. He looked familiar. Then she remembered, he had sat at a nearby table in the lunchroom and was being picked on by Ryan and Ethan. When Ryan kicked him, she remembered the look on Michael's face; he was furious and his teeth were clenched. He couldn't retaliate because he was outnumbered. Becca was so concerned with Kelly and didn't interfere. But she knew this poor kid was being bullied too.

Michael was small and slender and, of course, wore glasses. *Why is it that kids who wear glasses get picked on?* She opened her note pad and jotted Ryan and Ethan's names. Next to Ryan's name, she wrote *bad complexion* and next to Ethan's she wrote *sexual* because whenever he had something to say, it was of a sexual nature.

Michael James was now in his element. In this class, he was answering questions and appeared to be very bright in math.

Kelly also participated. *What a bright young woman. It's a shame she's being bullied by these lowlifes.* Becca always gave everyone the benefit of the doubt, and tried not to be opinionated. However, in this case she thought otherwise.

As Michael glanced over at Becca again, she smiled at him. He put his head down and blushed.

When the class was over, she told Kelly she wanted to talk to Michael. They waited for him by the door.

"Hi. I heard the teacher call you Michael, I'm Becca. Do you know Kelly?" The boy nodded. "You're really smart," Becca said. "I wish I knew more about algebra."

He looked at her as though she had four heads. *Wow, this poor kid probably never had anyone compliment him. He's so used to being harassed.*

All he could say was, "Thanks."

"I'm sorry you were hassled by those jerks in the cafeteria," said Becca. "I understand they were picking on Kelly the other day. Did you see what happened?"

Michael looked from Kelly to Becca and shrugged. He seemed reluctant to talk, as was Kelly. Becca thought the bullying must terrify both.

"I'm upset about those kids bothering you and Kelly. I'd like to help."

Again, Michael had a strange look on his face as though Becca were an alien. He scrunched his eyebrows and scratched his head.

"You can sit with us in the cafeteria tomorrow. You know; strength in numbers." Becca didn't tell him she was Kelly's Guardian ad-litem. She wanted him to think she was one of the students. He nodded, pursed his lips, and walked away not giving any indication whether he would join them or not.

Becca looked at her watch. It was five minutes to three. Eric would be in the parking lot. She wondered if Dylan would be waiting for her too.

Kelly didn't say anything. Her eyes darted with worry as though she read Becca's mind.

Outside, at the bottom of the steps, Becca saw the three boys huddled around Dylan. He jerked his head at her, and they all looked up and yelled obscenities. She and Kelly had to pass the boys to get to the parking lot where she hoped Eric waited. Becca didn't know what she should do. She knew Dylan was bad news according to Mrs. Franklin. Her sole responsibility now was Kelly. But she was also concerned for her own safety.

———◆———

Dylan looked up at Becca and Kelly. His anger raged inside. If you weren't for him, you were the enemy, and he saw Becca as the enemy. His mind raced with ways he could hurt her and make her sorry for treating him the way she did.

"Wow, that blonde girl is fi…ne," said Ethan. "She's probably on the DLF. I'd like to hit that some time."

"Ethan, is that all you think about?" said Ryan.

"Maybe if *you* get some, your face will clear up," said Ethan.

The other three laughed and fist bumped.

"Dylan, why are you wasting your time with her?" Tony asked. "What did you text in English? I saw you take your phone out and look at her."

"I don't like the way she dissed me in the lunchroom. When I asked for her name, she looked at me like she didn't give a crap's ass. She's hangin' out with that freakin' ratchet face, a nobody who doesn't deserve to live."

"So what did you say?" asked Ethan.

"I told the bitch to watch her back."

All three said, "Ooooh."

"I feel sorry for that bitch," said Tony.

"Hey, there's that nerd from the lunchroom," Tony said, pointing to Michael James, who waited for the bus a few feet away.

"I'll bet he needs to get some too." Tony yelled to Michael, "Hey, goggle face, what did I tell you about breathing my air. Don't dump your nerd germs in my space."

Michael lowered his head and moved farther away.

"You're still too close."

The other boys laughed. "He's really scared," said Ryan. "Look at his face."

Tony lost interest in Michael when the girls from the lunchroom joined them.

Lorraine, who was crazy about Dylan, sidled up to him, and said, "What do you think of the chick who sat with frog girl in the lunchroom?" She was baiting him. "She looks like a ho." She turned around and looked up at Kelly and Becca waiting on top of the steps. "Imagine sitting with that creepy girl who never talks. She'd rather be friends with her than with us." She took out her cell phone and began texting. "I'm telling the ugly frog girl to stay home tomorrow because the school is being fumigated from her germs."

They all laughed.

Tony started propositioning the girls. They teased back. All forgot about Becca, all except Dylan, who continued to stare at her like a beast of prey.

Becca looked out at the parking lot to see if she could see Eric. She occasionally glanced at the boys teasing Michael and flirting with the girls. Even though Dylan seemed to be engaged in their company, he never kept his eyes from her for more than a few seconds. She wanted to walk down the steps and into the parking lot but was afraid of what Dylan would do. He couldn't be trusted, especially, after the text message she assumed he wrote.

Kelly tapped Becca on the shoulder and pointed to Eric striding toward them. Becca waved with relief. Eric waved back as he walked closer, passing Dylan and the others.

"Why are you waiting up here? I thought I told you to meet me in the parking lot," Eric said. Then he smiled at Kelly. "Hi, Kelly." She smiled back but didn't say a word.

Becca was so happy to see Eric that she almost hugged him. "Let's go. I'll tell you later."

The three went down the steps and past the bullies. All of them shouted remarks.

"Blondie and Froggie have a boyfriend."

Tony gyrated and said, "Oooh."

Eric said, "Wow, it's been a long time."

As they passed, Dylan locked eyes with Becca. If looks could be daggers, she would be dead. A chill went through her as she thought of the text.

WHEN THEY PASSED DYLAN AND his crew, Eric noticed the look on both Kelly and Becca's face. Kelly flashed a frightened look at Eric, and Becca opened her eyes wide and slightly shook her head as if to say, "Don't ask." Because Eric knew why Becca was there, he didn't ask any questions during the ride home to Kelly's house. Becca and Kelly sat together in the back seat.

"Did I tell you how nice you look today, Kelly?" said Eric, looking at her in his rearview mirror.

Kelly blushed, lowered her eyes, and nodded. Then she looked at Becca and said, "I'm glad Becca was there today."

Becca patted her hand and said, "I'm glad too. And I'll be with you tomorrow."

She asked Eric general questions about the office. "When is Mr. Klein coming in? Please make sure it's in the afternoon so I can be present."

"Don't worry. We'll make sure of that." He made some other small talk about what was happening with some of their other cases. They soon approached Kelly's home. Becca walked her to the door. Her mother answered, and Becca told her they would pick her up again tomorrow. Becca hugged Kelly and said, "I'll see you tomorrow."

When she got back in the car, Eric said, "So?"

Becca closed her eyes tightly and heaved a sigh.

"That bad, eh." Eric drove and turned to look at her.

"Worse," said Becca. She continued to tell Eric what she encountered in the lunchroom. When she got to the text, he slammed on the brakes, and pulled over to the side of the road.

He turned to look at her. "What! I'm pulling you off this case. We'll have Officer Regino look into it. We can catch the bullies some other way."

"No, Eric. They're very clever. They have a ringleader who needs to be stopped. I must admit, I'm a little scared, but this is the only way to catch them and put an end to it." Eric stared at her for several seconds before he continued driving again. He listened as she told him about the rest of the day.

Eric kept shaking his head in disbelief. "This is worse than I thought."

Becca assured him she knew what she was doing and wanted to stay on the case. Eric reluctantly agreed.

———————

When Becca got to the office, there was a message from Jason Regino. He wanted to know how her day went. Before she could call him, she wanted to check on Kelly. She called, and her mother answered.

"Hi, Mrs. Richards, how's Kelly doing?"

"Thank you for volunteering to do this; it means so much to us. She feels safe with you there." Mrs. Richards hesitated and Becca could hear a slight sob on the other end. "She told me how you stood up to those terrible boys. I have her old cell phone, and someone is still texting her horrible things. I took it away when she was showing signs of deep depression. As I told Mr. Jefferies in the office, I keep it for proof of the harassment."

"The next time you come into the office, I'd like to see the messages."

"Do you want to talk to Kelly?" asked Mrs. Richards.

"No, that's okay. I just wanted to see how she's doing. I'll pick her up tomorrow morning."

"Thank you for calling, Miss Curtis, I'm so glad we hired your firm."

"Please, call me Becca. We'll get to the bottom of this, and you can have your happy child again."

When Becca hung up, she wondered if she could back up her statement to Mrs. Richards. Today was rough. Somehow, with unbelievable luck, she avoided Dylan. She didn't know about tomorrow. She was anxious to get to her computer to document that day's experience and list the names of the boys. She wanted to turn her report over to Eric as soon as possible. But before she started, she had to call Jason.

"Hi, Jason, I just got your message."

"Thanks for calling me back. I was anxious to find out how you made out. I was thinking about you all day."

"I can tell you that it was quite an experience. The six years difference made me feel far removed from the kids today. They actually speak a different language."

"I know what you mean. I deal with them every day. Mrs. Franklin called the precinct to ask for more officers at the school tomorrow. I volunteered. So I guess I'll see you in the cafeteria."

"Oh, that's great, Jason, because..." She proceeded to tell him what happened at school.

"Now I know why Mrs. Franklin asked for more officers. I'll surely keep an eye on you two."

"Just be careful, I want to catch those bullies in the act so we can nail them." She was happy Jason was going to be in the cafeteria. She really worried about Dylan.

"Hey, do you have school tonight?" Jason asked.

"Not tonight. Why?"

"I thought we could try that nice Italian restaurant down the street from your office. I hear they have great food. We could talk some more about the case."

Is he asking for a date? Or does he just want to talk about the case? Becca didn't know what to think.

"I...I..." Becca hesitated. She was tired and wanted to go home, take a nice hot bath, and chat with her parents, who always gave her comfort. She knew she couldn't discuss all the details with them, especially the text. They would worry.

As if he'd read her mind he said, "I know you're tired and you've had a hard day. I'll get you home early, I promise. Say yes." Jason was quite persuasive.

"Okay, pick me up at five."

After they hung up, Becca started typing her notes. She tried not to leave anything out.

While Eric worked in his office, he had the door open and could see the back of Becca's head. She was typing away. He thought about the assignment and still worried her life was in danger.

Maybe I should take her off the case. I would never forgive myself if she got hurt. But she's headstrong. She wants to do it. We'll try one more day. Tomorrow is Friday. She'll have the weekend to think it over.

Eric thought about his father and what action he would have taken in this case. He missed him at a time like this and hoped he was doing the right thing. He thought about Kelly. He didn't want her to be another statistic. As soon as Becca gave him her report, he'd move ahead with the preparations for suing the parents of the bullies. *We need to help that kid and her parents. Thanks, Dad. I know what you would do!*

JASON ARRIVED PROMPTLY AT FIVE. Becca had typed her notes and had given them to Eric. She wanted to wait for him to finish reading them before she left for the day.

Becca told the receptionist, "Please tell Officer Regino I'll be out in a few minutes." She went into Eric's office to tell him she was leaving and asked if there were any instructions for tomorrow.

He looked up from the notes and blinked a few times. "Wow, we could probably nail these kids based on the information you wrote."

"Yes, I know, but I want to get a few more witnesses to make an iron-clad case." Becca was adamant.

"Okay, come in early, and I'll take both of you to school. I want to give this report to Mrs. Franklin. Don't be surprised if, after she reads it, she pulls those kids out of class and suspends them."

"Please tell her to give me one more day," Becca said. "I know I'll have much more ammunition. Besides, Jason Regino is assigned to the cafeteria tomorrow. I'll feel safe with him there."

"How did that happen?" Eric said curiously.

"Mrs. Franklin called the precinct. I guess she was worried when she read the text Dylan wrote."

"And she had every right to be. Curtis, I hope you know what you're doing?"

"One more day, Eric, I promise. I'll see you tomorrow."

"Okay, have a good evening. I know you don't have school tonight so you can get rest."

"Yes, I will. I'm having dinner with Jason at that Italian restaurant down the street."

"Oh." Eric began organizing his desk and, without looking at Becca, said, "Have a good time."

"Thanks." As if she needed to justify dinner with Jason, she said, "We want to strategize for tomorrow."

Eric looked up, raised an eyebrow, and murmured, "Mmmm."

Becca gathered her cell and purse and started towards the reception area. *What was that all about? It's just dinner.*

She reached the reception area and saw Jason sitting, reading a magazine. He wore his civilian clothing: jeans and a white, collared shirt. Becca thought he looked just as good in regular clothes as he did in his uniform. His muscles still bulged under his shirt. When he looked up and saw her, he stood and said, "Hi. Ready?"

Becca suddenly felt butterflies in her stomach. "Yes, and I'm starving." She tried to appear normal, but deep down she was beginning to feel something more than friendship for Jason.

———◆———

When they arrived at the restaurant, it wasn't crowded, and the hostess directed them to a private table off to the side. Becca noticed soft music playing in the background. It was very relaxing, almost romantic. "This is nice. I've never been here before. Do you eat here often?" Becca asked.

"No, but they have a reputation for good food. It's quiet, so we can talk."

"Yes. After the stressful day I've had, this is great."

The waiter stood at the table to take their drink orders. "Something to drink, signora? For you, signore?"

"Why don't you have a glass of wine," said Jason, "I think you need it."

"You're right. I'll have a glass of Merlot."

"Make that two."

"He called me signora. If I'm not mistaken, that means Mrs."

Does he think we're married?

"He probably calls all the ladies signora," said Jason. "This is an Italian restaurant."

"I guess so," said Becca.

"I can't get over that kid…what did you say his name was…Dylan?"

Becca nodded. "Yes, Dylan. At least I believe it was him."

"What do you mean?" asked Jason.

"Of course, I don't know if the text came from him. However, after I read it I looked directly at him, and he slid his hand across his throat as though he were cutting, so I believe it was him."

"Oh yeah, then it was him alright," said Jason. "I run into punks like that all the time. Let me see the phone number. I'll see if I can find out who it belongs to. I'll be in the cafeteria tomorrow and will make sure he doesn't do anything stupid."

"I would like to catch those bullies in the act so we have more evidence for the school, and the court. As far as I know, there are four boys and two girls who are terrorizing Kelly and a boy named Michael James. I saw two of the boys throw Michael's lunch on the floor. I can't tell you how it angered me." Becca bit her lip and shook her head. "I'm hoping he will agree to make a statement regarding *his* bullying."

"Remember, I was also a recipient of such torture." Jason sat up in his chair. "That's why I want to help these kids as much as I can. I hope Michael will cooperate too."

"I'm so happy you're going to be in the cafeteria tomorrow." Realizing he may catch on that her excitement was due to more than just his protection, she lowered her eyes and blushed. She was glad the waiter came over with their drinks and was ready for their order.

"Becca, why don't you try the ravioli? You can have a salad too."

She was about to pass on the pasta when she decided to enjoy the evening, the company, and the food. "Why not? Yes, I'll have the ravioli."

Jason said, "Make that two."

They found themselves forgetting about the bullying and exchanged stories of their past. Jason told Becca his favorite things to do. Surprised, she liked the same. He told her he wanted to travel and see the world, and that he loved swimming, hiking, and biking. That came as no surprise. He was in excellent physical condition. She always thought of herself as athletic and a nature lover, but he surpassed her.

Their food arrived while they were deep in conversation. The waiter put the plates in front of them and said, "Buon appetito."

They didn't miss a beat and kept their conversation going. At one point, Jason looked deeply into her eyes and lightly touched her hand that was resting on the table. She should have been embarrassed, but wasn't. She just stared back. While she enjoyed the food, later she could hardly remember eating. Jason was everything she wanted in a man. She couldn't believe how drawn to him she was in such short a time.

———◆———

It was eight o'clock when Becca got home. Jason was right; the dinner was relaxing after the horrendous day. She and Jason had talked more about their personal lives than the case. She was happy she was going to see him tomorrow, even under dire circumstances.

Her parents asked her some questions, and she was careful not to worry them. She told them about Shakespeare and *Hamlet* and wondered if she could still recite the soliloquy. Her father began and got half way through. "That's great, Dad. I'm not sure I could get that far." They all laughed, and she was happy she didn't alarm them. Of course, she never mentioned the text.

———◆———

After dropping Becca off at her house, Jason thought of the wonderful evening he had with her. He knew he was falling for her and hoped she felt the same. But he couldn't forget the danger she was in. He didn't tell her that Mrs. Franklin requested a male undercover police officer to follow Dylan around for Becca's protection. It would be someone young enough to pass as a high school student. Both he and the principal didn't want to take any chances with Becca's safety. They knew the text was serious. The officer would follow Dylan around, and Jason would protect her in the cafeteria.

I hope she gets the proof she needs tomorrow. Each day places her in harm's way. Jason found himself caring deeply for Becca.

CHAPTER 20

BECCA WANTED TO GET A good night's sleep. She had a big day ahead of her. She took a warm bath and felt relaxed and ready for bed. Even though she was threatened by Dylan, all she could think about was the wonderful evening she just had with Jason and hoped there would be more. She closed her eyes and was soon sound asleep.

When she woke the next morning, Becca recalled her dream where she walked alone in the park amid a field of red and pink tulips on a beautiful sun-shiny day. The clouds were low and billowy. She could almost touch them. A slight breeze blew through the trees as they cast shadows from the sun. She took a breath and could smell the flowers and the fresh air. As she continued to walk, a hill appeared in the distance. Someone was standing on top. She was too far away to make out the figure. With broad shoulders, flat chest and small hips, it appeared to be a male. She felt compelled to walk toward the hill. The figure waved, gesturing to join him. With a happy feeling in her heart, she walked closer to the hill. Someone tapped her on the shoulder. Turning, she was shocked to see Dylan. He had an evil grin on his face. His eyes narrowed, and he threw his head back as he let out a sinister laugh. Frightened, she pulled away and started running toward the hill. The figure waved motioning her to hurry. Dylan kept running too. She ran as fast as she could, but he kept up with her, only inches away. She was breathing heavily and could feel her heart pound in her chest. The person on the hill urged her on. When she reached the hill, she climbed faster and higher. Dylan slightly behind her shouted terrible things. He called her names, the same ones they called Kelly: ho, slut, and ratchet face. He indicated cutting her throat as he did in class after he sent the text. She got closer and closer, and was almost able to see the figure still waving to her when her alarm went off. She woke with a start and sat up in bed.

Who was that person on the hill? She shook her head. *Now Dylan is invading my dreams as well as my life. I'll have to be careful today.*

—◆—

She wanted to get to the office early. She dressed again in jeans and T-shirt, and swept her hair into a ponytail. With little make-up, she looked every bit the teenager. When she went in for breakfast, her mother did a double take. "You look more like a student than a Guardian ad Litem," her mother said as she busied herself in the kitchen. "How much longer will you accompany Kelly?"

"I'm hoping today will be the last day. There's another student being bullied by the same group. I'm counting on him to help. I'm going to talk to him today." Becca didn't want to give her mother any further details that might worry her. If she knew about the text, she would insist Becca step down and let the proper authorities handle it.

Becca ate a light breakfast, said her goodbyes, and left for work. While driving, she recalled the previous day and worried about her encounters with Dylan. The day before, Kelly let her know that Ryan and Ethan were in her biology class and that Dylan was only in English. That was good news; however, would he try to stalk her between classes? She remembered the dream and thought how he even stalked her dreams. Having Jason in the cafeteria made her feel safe. Still, she thought, *I have to make progress today. My only hope is to have Michael testify to the bullying.* She wondered how she would go about that. She knew he was also afraid of the four boys. She had to gain his confidence and convince him to help.

———•———

Eric arrived before Becca and was on the phone with Mrs. Franklin. She informed him that a male officer, posing as a student, would shadow Dylan. They didn't want to alert Becca for fear she would not act normal around Kelly. Dylan and his friends had to be caught in the act of bullying so they would have an ironclad case. After he hung up with Mrs. Franklin, Eric saw Becca come in and sit at her desk. He stepped out of his office.

"Hi. How do you feel today?"

Becca looked up at Eric and shrugged her shoulders. "Excited? Scared?"

Eric looked at her with concern. "Scared?"

"Well, I would be lying if I said otherwise, but don't worry, I think we're making headway. Having Jason Regino there makes me feel better."

Eric wished he could put her mind at ease and tell her about the undercover police officer. But he only looked at her and said, "As soon as you're ready, we'll go and pick up Kelly."

"Give me a few minutes to coordinate with Carolyn." Becca wanted to make sure her work was being covered while she was with Kelly at school.

When they arrived at her house, Kelly seemed better than she had been the day before. She actually smiled at them and said, "Good morning."

"Well, good morning to you. Are you ready for another day with your Guardian ad Litem?" Eric said in a lighthearted and friendly voice.

Once at the school, Eric went to see Mrs. Franklin to give her Becca's report. The girls went to Kelly's first class, Ancient History.

"Michael James is in this class," Kelly told Becca.

"I'll be glad to see him," Becca said. "I want to invite him to sit with us at lunch again."

Kelly nodded her head. Becca suspected she liked Michael.

The teacher began her lesson. Again, Michael knew all the answers. Becca realized this boy was extremely intelligent and had a lot to offer society when he grew up. But kids like Dylan and his crew would destroy his self-esteem. Even Kelly was participating in the class feeling comfortable without the bullying.

He needs my help as much as Kelly does. How can I get to him? What do I say? He needs someone to tell him he's worthy.

It was just like Becca, going over and beyond her duties. She was there as a Guardian ad Litem for Kelly. But now her heart and instincts told her to include Michael in her mission to stop the bullying.

When the class was over, Becca walked over to Michael as he gathered his books. "Michael, Kelly, and I are eating alone today. Why don't you sit with us at lunch? Maybe those kids won't bother us if we're all together."

He looked at her with squinted eyes, picked up his books, and walked away.

Becca shouted, "So is that a yes?"

He turned and slowly nodded his head.

"Great. See you then." She looked at Kelly and winked.

CHAPTER 21

Tᴍ Cᴀʟʟᴏᴡᴀʏ ʜᴀᴅ ᴊᴜsᴛ sᴛᴀʀᴛᴇᴅ with the police force six months ago. Up until last week, he successfully went undercover to expose some gang members who were deep into drugs. Tim was tall, thin, and wiry, and even though he was twenty-four, he was able to look every bit the part of a teenager. His lanky stature was deceiving. He could take down a person bigger than him with one fell swoop.

Today, his assignment was to follow Dylan Baker. He had been briefed the day before at the precinct and early that morning in Mrs. Franklin's office. Although he could talk the jive of a teenager, he was quite a serious police officer. Jason had suggested him to Mrs. Franklin.

At the lockers, Tim pretended to take out some books while listening to Dylan's conversation with his three friends.

"Who has class with Froggie and Blondie today? I need to re-arrange their faces."

"They're in our biology, fourth-period class," said Ryan.

"That's too late. Where are they now?" Dylan was asking the three.

They all shrugged. "Don't know," said Ryan.

"Ah, I guess I'll have to wait until lunch period. Make sure you dipshits get there early. We're going to have some fun," Dylan said with a devious smile.

Tim listened. He knew he had to stick close to Dylan. His instincts told him he was dangerous. Tim made sure he was always far enough away not to draw suspicion, but close enough to stop any threatening act.

Kelly's next class was geography. It was one of Becca's favorite classes in high school. She always thought one day she would travel the world and visit the places she'd studied. She loved the cultures, architecture, and fashion design that influenced the modern world.

Becca was beginning to enjoy being back in high school, especially seeing how Kelly and Michael participated in the last two classes without someone putting them down. They were two intelligent teenagers who could develop into responsible adults to help mold and develop the future of our society. Becca couldn't help thinking what a contribution they could make.

As they walked to class, she pleasantly chatted with Kelly. In the middle of their conversation, Kelly stopped talking—and walking. It took Becca a moment to realize Kelly lagged behind. Turning back to her, she followed Kelly's line of sight as she stared at Lorraine who was slightly ahead of them.

"What's wrong?" Becca asked.

"I forgot she's in my geography class." Kelly knitted her eyebrows and chewed her bottom lip.

"It's okay. That's why I'm here, to see that no one bothers you. Don't worry." Becca flashed Kelly her widest grin.

Kelly smiled back, and they resumed walking.

In class, the students were talking and laughing. Something made of paper flew through the air and almost hit Becca. She ducked and glanced around to see where it came from. A boy laughed and pointed at her. She picked the paper up, holding her breath as she opened it. It was blank. The boy was just being a jerk. Becca let out a huge sigh of relief.

After she took her letter of introduction to the teacher, Becca sat next to Kelly. When she spotted Lorraine, who reminded Becca of all that Dylan stood for, she felt a tightening in her chest. In a few hours, she would confront him in the lunchroom. She had to be brave for Kelly's sake. It wasn't so much that she was afraid of Lorraine. It was what she represented: psycho Dylan and his weird friends.

Lorraine was busy talking to another girl and didn't see her. But it was only a matter of time.

Then it happened.

Lorraine spotted them when she turned to talk to a girl behind her. She glared at Becca. Then she mouthed, "You bitch." Becca turned and smiled at Kelly but could still feel Lorraine's penetrating stare.

Kelly stiffened. Becca shook her head and quietly said, "It's okay."

All during class Lorraine kept turning to glare at her. At one point, the teacher called to her, "Lorraine, what's so interesting behind you? I'm teaching the class up front."

Becca could tell Lorraine was angry. If she called her a bitch from across the room, she could only imagine what other choice words she had for her.

When the bell rang, Becca and Kelly left quickly to avoid Lorraine. They'd only gotten halfway down the hall when Lorraine pushed her way through the crowd and caught up with them, grabbing Becca's shoulder.

"You skank ho retarded bitch! Don't let me catch you near Dylan or I'll pull that bleached blonde hair outta your head."

Becca shrugged off Lorraine's hold. "Listen, girl. You better keep your guy on a short leash. He's the one bothering me. I have no dibs on him."

"He's always talking about you. He's pissed at you cause you dissed him in the lunchroom. Nobody does that to Dylan Baker," Lorraine shouted.

"Then, if *you* have dibs on him, you better set him straight. He's not my type." Becca winked at Kelly to lighten the situation and kept walking as she spoke to Lorraine. "So he's all yours."

Lorraine stopped, waved her fist, and said, "You better watch your ass in the lunchroom; you and your frog face friend."

Becca told Kelly to ignore Lorraine's threats. "She's really jealous isn't she? Why would she fight for a guy like that?" Then she giggled to hide her worry that Dylan would start something in the cafeteria. "Okay, where to now?"

Kelly's eyes twinkled. "Now we go to my favorite class. Biology." But the sparkle left when she lowered her head and said, "Those awful boys are in this class."

"You mean Ryan and Ethan, Dylan's friends?"

"Yes." Kelly kept her head down.

From somewhere deep inside, Becca drew on her strength. She knew she had to be brave to endure the next few hours. Dylan was unpredictable, and Becca had to be prepared to protect Kelly as well as herself.

She heard her father's voice in her head. *Remember, Rebecca Rose. You're on eagle's wings. He's holding you in the palm of His hands.*

"Listen, Kelly, we're going to ignore those jerks. We had a pleasant morning. Leave everything to me. I know you love your biology class. You can probably teach me a few things. Let's just concentrate on the lesson. Did you say Michael James is in this class, too?"

Kelly looked up and nodded her head. The twinkle came back.

"Good. I'm looking forward to seeing him again."

Kelly blushed and said, "Me too."

The classroom impressed Becca. The tables were set up like a lab. There were test tube racks, glass beakers, Bunsen burners, and microscopes. Michael was already at one of the tables. Becca walked over to him, and Kelly followed. "Can we sit at your table? I'm learning so much from you and Kelly. You guys are so smart."

Michael lowered his head. Becca could swear that Michael blushed. "Yeah, better you two than those other jerks."

CHAPTER 22

<hr>

AFTER BECCA GAVE HER NOTE to the teacher, she resumed her place at the table with Kelly and Michael. Becca was surprised to see Kelly talking to Michael. She realized they had so much in common.

The teacher went on with the lesson, and Kelly and Michael were in their element. When the teacher turned his back to write on the blackboard, Ethan came over and whispered in Kelly's ear. Instinctively, Becca grabbed his arm and practically swung him across the room. He let out a hearty laugh that made the teacher turn around. Ethan just shook his head and shrugged. The teacher resumed writing on the board.

While the incident was going on, Michael stepped in front of Kelly as if to protect her. He kept turning around to see that Ethan stayed at his table. Ryan noticed him and gave him the finger.

Then Ethan looked directly at Becca, bobbed his head up and down and said in a low voice, "Hey, Blondie, Dylan's gonna catch you later."

Becca knew there would be trouble, but she was prepared. Knowing that Jason would be in the cafeteria gave her confidence.

When the class was over, Becca lingered with Kelly and Michael. She kept asking questions about the lesson. Both Kelly and Michael were all too happy to help her. She opened her notebook and pretended to write down their answers, but she was actually writing about the incident with Ethan.

When she thought Ethan and Ryan were gone, they packed up and headed for the door. Kelly smiled at Michael. "Remember, you said you would sit with us at lunch."

They walked a few feet outside the classroom toward the cafeteria when someone tapped Becca on the shoulder. Twisting to look, she saw her worst nightmare. There was Dylan strutting in the middle of Ryan, Ethan, and Tony. "Hey, Blondie. Going my way?"

Becca was shocked. *This is just like my dream. What do I do? What do I say? Strategize, Becca. Don't show you're scared. Think, girl, think!*

"We're headed to the principal's office." She thought that would confuse him.

"Why, have you been a naughty girl?" Dylan and his followers laughed.

Michael and Kelly appeared confused. Becca tapped on Kelly's arm as a sign to follow her lead. She knew Michael caught it too.

Dylan clamped his large hand, like a vise, around Becca's arm, pulling her away from Kelly and Michael. "I'll walk with you," he said in a fear-provoking voice. Becca had to act brave and not show any distress even though her insides were shaking. She knew that animals attack when you show fear; and she thought Dylan was an animal.

"Why did you send me that awful text? I thought you liked me." Becca tried to keep calm for Michael and Kelly's sake.

Dylan stopped walking, stared at her through narrowed eyes, and then loosened his grip on her arm. "Well, yesterday you pissed me off in the lunchroom. You didn't want to talk to me."

"I can't. I have strict parents." Becca was grasping at straws.

Dylan raised his eyebrows and curled his lips into a smile. "I'm glad you're here. Maybe we can hang out." He let go of her arm and his face relaxed. She felt the blood slowly circulating back in her veins.

———◆———

Michael was wide-eyed and confused. He didn't know whether to stay or run. But something in Becca made him want to stay to make sure no harm came to either her or Kelly.

Alert and perceptive, when Dylan grabbed Becca's arm, he immediately glanced around to see if there were any police officers. He saw a tall, tough-looking student a few feet behind them who seemed to be observing the situation. When Michael looked directly at him, the student jutted his jaw and winked. There was something about his gesture that comforted Michael, even though he was totally fearful of Dylan. No one else noticed him. They were concentrating on Dylan.

Michael despised Dylan, but he was too scared to stick up for himself. The four boys had been terrorizing him for the last three months. It was about the same time he saw them bullying Kelly. He liked Kelly and wanted to save her from their ruthless harassment, but he didn't think he was strong enough, mentally or physically.

When Dylan loosened his grip on Becca, Michael felt a sigh of relief. He was standing next to Kelly all the while and slightly touched her arm as if to say that all would be okay. He knew somehow Becca was there to help Kelly, but he wasn't sure how and why.

———◆———

Tim was behind them eyeing the situation. His remarkable instincts told him to wait when Dylan grabbed Becca's arm. He didn't want to blow his cover over just an arm grab. He was close enough to stop any harmful action. However, when Michael glanced around at him, he wanted to reassure him.

Earlier, the principal informed Tim that he was to try to escort Becca and Kelly to her office before lunch to go over what might happen in the cafeteria. He thought this would be a good time to do it.

From behind them he yelled, "Hey. Yo, Becca."

Becca turned immediately with a puzzled look on her face.

Dylan gave Tim a devious glare.

"Are you calling me?" Becca asked.

"Yeah, yeah, Mrs. Franklin wants to talk to you."

Becca gave him a curious glance and said, "I was just telling Dylan I was on my way to the principal's office". She looked at Dylan and shrugged.

"You must be in big trouble if Franklin wants to see you," said Tony with a gyrating gesture.

"Yeah, you and your friend." He pointed at Kelly. Quick on his toes, Tim thought of the boy with them and knew he needed help as well. "And you too. What's your name?"

"Me?" said Michael.

"Yeah, you."

"Michael."

"Yeah, she wants to see the three of you."

Dylan never wanted to be on the principal's radar, so he bobbed his head at his cronies to leave the scene. They left Tim and the three others quietly.

"What is this about?" said Becca.

Tim shrugged his shoulders. Still in undercover mode, he convinced all three he was a student. "C'mon let's go." Tim urged them toward the principal's office. "You know where it is, right?"

All three answered, "Yes."

"I'm outta here." Tim left them to continue his surveillance of Dylan.

CHAPTER 23

WHEN MRS. FRANKLIN MET WITH Officer Tim earlier, she told him that under no circumstances would she allow any harm come to Becca and Kelly. If he were to see any problem whatsoever, he was to send them to her office. However, she hid her surprise at seeing Michael. She trusted the officer and knew that if he sent Michael along, he had a reason. She asked Kelly and Michael to wait outside her office while she spoke with Becca.

Mrs. Franklin was careful not to reveal Officer Tim Calloway's identity. She agreed earlier with Officer Jason Regino that his presence would distract Becca and cause her to react differently to a situation. Although, a little displeased to think they were in some sort of trouble, she was glad their plan worked.

"Why did you send for me, Mrs. Franklin?" asked Becca. "Do you have any further instructions or information?"

"I'm concerned about the text. I want to reiterate that you must be careful in the cafeteria. These students can be dangerous."

"I just had a confrontation with Dylan," Becca said. "I think I can talk to him and win his confidence."

Mrs. Franklin sat erect in her chair. "What happened?"

"Nothing I couldn't handle. Dylan grabbed my arm, and then released it when I talked to him."

Shaking her head, Mrs. Franklin said, "These students have a history of violence. I realize that you want to document the bullying for your case. But you must understand that my concern is for the wellbeing of all the students." She nodded at Michael sitting outside. "Do you think he can help you with the case?"

Becca turned her head to look through the glass partition that separated the principal's office and the waiting room, then turned back to face Mrs. Franklin. "Definitely. I think he can play a big part in resolving this. I've seen them bully him as well as Kelly. We need him to cooperate and become a witness for us."

Becca told Mrs. Franklin of the incident with Lorraine.

"Lorraine is obsessed with Dylan," said the principal. "You know, she had a miscarriage a few months ago. We think Dylan was the father." Becca sat up in her seat and listened intently to Mrs. Franklin. "The school counselor had a session with her when she returned to school. Lorraine would not divulge the name of the father and the circumstances surrounding her miscarriage. She was approximately three months pregnant when she collapsed in school. When the school nurse examined her, she noticed bruises on her stomach and arms. She told the nurse that she fell at home. During the examination, she was writhing in pain. She was taken to the hospital where she later had a miscarriage."

Becca gasped, totally shocked by the story. Mrs. Franklin continued. "We were all suspicious of Dylan, but without her testimony or witnesses, there was nothing we could do."

"I can't believe she is still following him around," Becca said.

"Yes, this is what I'm trying to tell you. He's dangerous. And besides, you have to watch out for her friend, Tessa," said Mrs. Franklin.

"Really, I didn't see her do anything drastic." Becca had a look of surprise on her face.

"She's very sly and devious. She once put a match to another girl's hair. Fortunately, the girl pulled away fast enough to avoid burning her head."

"So why is she still here attending this school and not in Juvie?"

"Everyone's afraid of her," said Mrs. Franklin. "No one's admitted that they saw her put the match to the other student's head. It was the girl's word against Tessa's, who vehemently denied it. We couldn't do anything without a witness. Since that time, we watch her carefully. She knows this and is very careful with her threats."

"Mrs. Franklin," Becca said, "now do you see why I need concrete evidence to stop this outrageous bullying?"

Out in the waiting room Michael was curious about Becca being in the principal's office. "Do you think your friend is in trouble?"

"No," said Kelly. "She's a good friend and wants the principal to know what's happening with the kids that are bullying me."

Michael nodded his head and was contemplative. He knew that Becca was a caring person and hoped she could possibly help him as well. He was so tired of the bullying and wanted to do something. But he was afraid he was outnumbered. Becca wanted him to cooperate and help. Didn't she tell him there's strength in numbers? Now there were three of them. Was that enough to stop the bullying? "I wonder what they're talking about."

"I hope she's telling her what's going on," said Kelly. "By the way, what did you think of biology today?"

"You mean when stupid face came over to whisper in your ear?"

"Not that. He's an idiot. No, I meant the subject that the teacher wrote for tomorrow's assignment?"

"You mean how certain foods can boost your mood?"

"Yes," said Kelly, "how low glycemic foods can improve moods."

"Wow," said Michael, "we should slip some chocolate and turkey into Dylan's lunch."

Both laughed and the two continued to talk deeply about the lesson until Becca came out of the principal's office. "Hey you two, we're going to be late for lunch. Let's go."

———————

As they walked to the cafeteria, Michael and Kelly continued their conversation about biology. They even argued a little, which made Becca smile with a happy feeling in her heart. *How wonderful these two are when they're not confronted with awful bullies. With the support of eagle's wings, I'm going to help them out of this situation.*

When they reached the cafeteria, it was crowded and most of the students were already eating their lunch. Becca glanced around to find Jason. She saw a female officer walking around. She panicked. *Oh no, he's not here.* But when she continued to look around the room, she saw him on the other side disciplining some students. Her heart skipped a beat. She liked what she saw. *He really looks good in his uniform.* He was the essence of strength, not to mention handsome.

Becca searched for a table away from Dylan and his buddies. She spotted one and tapped Kelly on the shoulder. "Why don't you two grab your lunch, and I'll hold the table?"

"Do you want me to get you a tuna sandwich?" asked Kelly.

"Oh, sure, that sounds good."

The two walked off as Becca headed toward the table.

Tim Calloway was able to get a seat at a table near Dylan and his friends. He spotted the four boys sitting with Lorraine and Tessa. Ryan sat opposite Dylan while Lorraine sat next to him. As usual, Tony and Ethan were teasing the girls. He watched as Dylan followed Ryan's eyes moving to the other side of the room and was ready to step in at any sign of danger.

Dylan turned to see Becca sitting at the table alone. "She's by herself. Wonder if she got in trouble with the principal?" Dylan stared at Becca.

Lorraine was furious. "Why do you care about that ho? She's such a noob, already in trouble with the lady."

"Nah, the dickwads are on the lunch line." Tessa pointed to Kelly and Michael with trays in their hands.

Dylan turned to look. "Yep, I see them." Addressing Ryan he said, "Go check it out. See what happened."

Ryan stood up to leave.

"I'll go too," said Ethan. They walked over to Becca's table.

———◆———

Jason was discretely watching from across the room. He spotted all the action, the two walking over to Becca, and Kelly and Michael getting lunch. Even though he was ready to intervene at the first sign of trouble, Jason was grateful that Tim Calloway was at a nearby table.

Kelly and Michael got their lunch and started walking over to join Becca. When they passed Dylan, Tony, and the girls, Jason heard them shouting something but was too far away to hear. He slowly worked his way over to Becca's table.

———◆———

"Hey, Blondie, what's up? Did you get in trouble with the principal?" Ryan said as he sat opposite Becca. Ethan sat next to her.

Becca knew these two meant trouble. Disregarding his question, Becca said, "Sorry, guys, I'm expecting company. Can you move and make some room for my friends?"

"You mean those two nerds coming this way?" Ethan jutted his jaw.

Becca saw Kelly and Michael walking toward the table carrying their trays, while Jason inched his way over. "Yes, they went to get my lunch."

"You didn't answer me," said Ryan. "What about the principal?"

"She just wanted to know how the classes were going."

Before Kelly and Michael reached the table, Becca noticed Dylan, Lorraine, Tessa and Tony making their way over. Even though she felt trouble brewing, Becca realized this was the only way she could document the bullying. She was grateful Jason was in the room.

"What's going on here?" said Dylan.

Ryan answered, "The boss lady wanted to know about her classes."

"Oh really?" Dylan responded with a note of anger in his voice that made Becca and others afraid of him.

Ryan got up to let Dylan sit. Before Lorraine sat next to him, she gave Becca a shove and glared at her.

"My friends are coming," said Becca and looked in Kelly and Michael's direction. "Please make room for them."

"They can sit at the other table." Dylan pointed to the table he'd just left.

"No, I want them to sit here. You can go back to your table."

No one ever spoke to Dylan that way. He narrowed his eyes, and breathing through his nose like a bull taunted by a red cape, he said, "Move down and make room for her *friends*."

The way he said "friends" sent chills down Becca's spine.

———

CHAPTER 24

BEFORE REACHING THE TABLE, KELLY stopped when she saw Dylan and his friends sitting with Becca. Her face paled and she started to tremble. She turned to Michael and said, "I'm scared. I don't want to sit with them."

"Oh, don't worry," he said. "Look, there's a police officer going over to the table."

Michael's attempt at bravery didn't fool Kelly. "Michael," she said, "you look as scared as I am."

Michael just shook his head and resumed walking. Kelly trailed behind.

———

Jason was a few feet in front of Kelly and Michael when he reached the table. "How're you kids doing? Are you behaving?"

"Just having our lunch," said Dylan.

"Where *is* your lunch?" Jason asked.

"It's over there," Ryan said, pointing to the other table.

"Well, don't you think you should go back and finish your lunch?" Jason said then looked at Becca, "Where's yours?"

"My friends are bringing it." At that moment, Kelly and Michael arrived with their trays. "Here they are."

Both Kelly and Michael appeared reluctant to sit at the crowded table.

"Where are these two going to sit? Whoever left their lunch over there"—he pointed—"should go back to that table and let these kids sit with their friend," Jason said with authority.

"We have plenty of room, Officer. See, there's room for a few more." The tables were rectangular and seated ten. Dylan pointed to the empty seats at the end."

Jason glanced around and hesitated. "Okay… make room for these two." He turned to Michael and Kelly. "Enjoy your lunch."

He turned his back and continued his walk around the room, checking at each table as he passed so as not to cause suspicion.

———————

Tim Calloway first sat behind Dylan and his friends. When Dylan moved to sit with Becca, Tim inched his way over to a nearby table. He observed their conversation and saw Lorraine shove Becca. He carried a little pad and discretely jotted anything he thought pertinent to the case. When Jason asked the crew about their lunch, he had acknowledged Tim with a quick look, then returned his focus back to the table. Tim was glad Jason knew he was there.

As Tim casually ate his lunch, he did a good job of acting like a student. He carried on a brief conversation with a cute girl sitting next to him. Being a professional undercover officer, he could keep up his conversation with the girl and maintain his surveillance of the kids at the other table. He was briefed on Dylan, the three boys, and the two girls. He knew about Lorraine's miscarriage and Tessa's attempt to set fire to another girl's head. Ethan for his sexual offences, Ryan and Tony backing up Dylan in his bullying exploits. Each of them at one point had been in trouble. They were either suspended or served detention. He had his hands full and was glad to have Jason walking the room. He didn't personally know the female officer, only her name, Jody Hastings, and that she was unaware of the situation. He was ordered to observe and not step in unless there was a threat to the students' safety. His gut told him to be prepared.

⸺⬥⸺

Michael sat quietly, watching everything around him. He glanced over at Dylan, who sat at the head of the table next to Becca. Lorraine sat opposite them. Michael thought she did so in order to know everything Dylan was saying and doing. Her obsession with Dylan was sickening. Tessa sat next to her. Ethan, Tony, and Ryan were next to Tessa and opposite Kelly and Michael. He was grateful that Kelly sat between him and Becca. He hoped they could protect her from this sorry bunch. His eyes darted between the two police officers that were at opposite ends of the room. In the pit of his stomach, he had a twinge of regret that he agreed to join Becca and Kelly for lunch, but he'd started to care for Kelly and wanted to protect her.

Tony leaned over to Michael and said, "Pick up your sandwich; it's littering the floor."

Michael cringed. *No, not again.*

Tony was quick and knocked Michael's sandwich to the floor. Michael hesitated then bent down to pick it up, and Ryan kicked him. The girls laughed.

When Dylan heard the girls laughing, he said, "What's up?"

"Stupid ass keeps dropping his lunch," Tessa said, still laughing.

"That's not so funny," Becca said at hearing Tessa's response. "Too bad the kid doesn't have *his*

gang around him to throw *your* food on the floor."
She looked at Tony and Ryan as she spoke.

Even though Becca had tried to help him, Michael fumed, but didn't say a word, as usual. He was too scared to make a move and embarrassed it happened in front of Kelly.

———

Kelly felt contempt for these terrible kids, who had nothing better to do than to bully innocent students. Her heart went out to Michael when they pulled their lame prank again. After he picked up his sandwich, he looked pitiful. Kelly turned to him, pursed her lips, and tilted her head as if to say, "sorry." She wished she could say something like Becca did. Kelly knew Becca was not afraid, but concerned. Kelly began to get nervous. If they threw Michael's lunch on the floor, what would they try to do to her? She didn't know how much more she could take from these obnoxious kids. She wanted to leave.

Ethan sat directly opposite Kelly and said, "Hey, Froggie, how did it feel when you cut the frog's balls off? Did it turn you on?" Ethan appeared to enjoy taunting Kelly. "So what do you say? You and me get it on later?"

Tony stood and gyrated. They all laughed, except Becca, Kelly, and Michael.

Kelly grabbed Becca's arm and started to shake.

"Leave her alone," Becca said, "and go pick on one of your skank hos."

In spite of Becca coming to her defense, Kelly continued to shake.

Kelly was surprised when Michael jumped up too and said, "Leave her alone, man."

Dylan stood, walked over, and said, "You got something to say?" Michael just shrugged. It was obvious to Kelly that he was afraid of Dylan.

"She bothers us," said Dylan and dug his hand into Kelly's shoulder. "We told her to take her sorry ass outta here and croak. Why did she come back? We don't like her…or you…breathing our air. But we're being nice today; we let you sit with us." He continued to squeeze Kelly's shoulder as his face contorted into an evil glare.

Michael's face turned beet red. He took a deep breath as though he was ready to say something, but instead shook his head. Kelly knew he was frightened and couldn't help her.

———————

While Dylan was squeezing Kelly's shoulders, Becca wanted to push him away, but didn't knowing what repercussions it would cause. Instead, she grabbed Kelly's hand and stroked her arm. Knowing Dylan's reputation, she kept calm and hoped Jason was watching. She glanced in his direction and, as luck would have it, he was.

All Becca could say was, "Dylan, please leave her alone."

Kelly began to cry and started to hyperventilate. She was swaying in the seat.

"Look at her," Ryan taunted, "she's finally going to pass out and drop dead."

"Stop!" Becca was losing her patience. "Can't you see you're scaring her?" Kelly was seriously wobbling. Becca glanced around and saw the female officer rush toward them.

Tim Calloway noticed Officer Jody Hastings approaching and watched, ready to intercede if necessary.

"What's going on here?" said Officer Hastings. She went over to Kelly, who looked terrible as she reeled and batted her eyes. "Are you ill?" she asked, but it was obvious Kelly was in distress.

With his hand still on Kelly's shoulder, Dylan said through gritted teeth, "Nah, she's okay. We're friends, just having fun."

Kelly was unable to talk. She looked up at the officer and mouthed the word "help." She started to sway. Her breathing became erratic.

Officer Hastings turned to Dylan. "Take your arm off her," she demanded and gave Dylan a hard shove. Without the support of Dylan's hold, Kelly wobbled, closed her eyes, and started to slip off her chair.

Tim was on the edge of his seat as he watched Dylan lose his balance and fall. He glanced at Jason walking briskly toward them with a worried look on his face.

Before Kelly hit the floor, Officer Hastings bent over to catch her.

Dylan fumed thinking a *lady* officer shoved him. He was boiling inside and his animal instincts made him want to retaliate. No one ever shoved him and got away with it, especially a female. His hands were clenched. This time, he thought he wouldn't be able to control his temper and might punch her in the face. When the officer bent over to catch Kelly, the snap on her holster had popped open. Dylan smiled at the full access to her weapon. In his anger, he instinctively reached over and pulled the gun out of the holster.

Everything happened so fast; Everyone's eyes were on Kelly. No one realized he had taken the gun.

Except Jason. He rushed across the room when he saw Dylan reach for the gun. This suddenly became a serious situation. He craned his head to see past students blocking his view as Officer Hasting worked to keep Kelly from falling and helped her back into her seat next to Michael.

It wasn't until the officer straightened and stepped aside that Jason saw Dylan holding the gun with two hands and pointing it at Officer Hastings.

C H A P T E R 2 5

——◆——

OH NO, DYLAN'S HOLDING A gun!

From his viewpoint, Officer Tim Calloway didn't see Dylan grab the gun. When he stood to get a better look, he saw the dilemma.

Thinking quickly, he strode over and yelled, "He's got a gun! He's got a gun!" Knowing this would cause the students to panic and run, he thought at least they would be safe.

The students jumped up, yelled, screamed, and rushed into Jason as he tried to reach the table. Jason's only choice was to herd them out safely.

"Put the gun down. You don't want to do this. You'll be in a lot of trouble," Officer Hastings said as she held her hands up and talked calmly to Dylan.

"Shut up, bitch. You shouldn't have pushed me. Kneel down on the ground and tell me you're sorry." He pointed the gun at her.

In an angry voice, she said, "I'm sorry."

Dylan yelled, "Louder, I can't hear you."

"I'M SORRY," Officer Hastings repeated.

"Don't any of you move, including you, long streak," Dylan said, motioning Tim to sit. "You rat out. I should shoot you now for telling that I got a gun." He then turned to Becca. "See, I don't need a gang to protect me, I have this gun."

Glad he was able to alert the kids by shouting about the gun, Tim now had to remain calm and not irritate Dylan. Tim had a P380 hidden in his sock and hoped he didn't have to use it to stop a crazy kid from shooting someone.

As Dylan pointed the gun around the table, his friends made comments.

"Yeah, Dylan, you're the man," said Ethan.

"Way to go, Dylan," said Tony and Ryan. Even though they praised him, their faces showed fear.

"Woo, woo." Tessa was the only one who cheered.

Lorraine just looked at Dylan in awe. In her eyes, he could do no wrong.

Dylan puffed out his chest and held the gun steadily with both hands. He continued to point the gun around the table, then back at Hastings kneeling on the floor.

Kelly woke from her fainting spell and let out a frightening scream when she saw Dylan holding the gun.

He looked at her and said, "Calm down, you freakin' loser before I blast your brains out." His eyes were dark and menacing as he held onto the gun.

<hr>

Becca's head reeled. Her adrenalin caused her heart to pound. She looked for Jason and saw him ushering the students out safely. He glanced at her and nodded, letting her know he would be over as soon as the students were safe. She tried her best to stay calm. While her heart raced, she wanted to think of something to say to Dylan to make him give up the gun. She worried about Kelly. *The poor kid has been through so much, now this.*

Jason finished herding all the students to safety; he walked over to the table with his arms raised. "You don't want to do that. Why don't you give me the gun so we can all leave this room peacefully?"

Dylan pointed the gun at Jason. "As a matter of fact, Officer, I'll take your gun too. NOW."

Jason did as he was told. He had to surrender his gun to Dylan in order to save the others. With his left hand held up, he undid the snap with his right hand and very carefully took out his weapon and handed it to him. Dylan grabbed it and tucked it in his pants.

"Why did you come back you asshole? You could've left with the others." Dylan snarled at Jason.

"I'm here to uphold the law and ensure the safety of all the students… including you. *All* of you are my priority," Jason said as he nodded to everyone at the table.

Dylan laughed. It was maniacal and scary. His friends were restless in their seats, glancing at each other, waiting for him to make a move.

Tim sat there with many thoughts swimming around. Earlier today, he was assigned to the case at Jason's request. None of the students knew Tim Calloway was an undercover officer who carried a concealed weapon. Because of his training, Tim knew Dylan was dangerous and could possibly shoot and kill someone. He had to be careful how he handled Dylan. Both he and Jason were communicating with their eyes. When Jason glanced at him, Tim gave him a slight nod, indicating that he was going to try something.

"Wow, man," Tim said to Dylan. He leaned over to get a better look at the gun. "I ain't never seen a gun up close." He wanted to see if the load chamber indicator was revealed. It was. The gun was chambered and the trigger was in the center ready to shoot. *Not good!* "What kind do you think it is?"

"It's a Glock, you asshole."

"Glock?" Tim acted dumb.

"Yeah, bird brain." Dylan pointed the gun at Tim.

Tim raised his arms and shook his head. "What're you planning to do? Shoot us all? Man, you could be in a lot of trouble for this. I had a friend who tried to pull a gun on a cop. He's in jail now. I don't play with guns. People can get hurt. I like the weed. It's much safer."

"Shut up, you bake out." Dylan yelled. "Anyone else got any ideas?" He moved the gun around the table and paced back and forth.

Tim knew he had to think fast. He could see Dylan was irritated. "Hey, calm down, calm down." Tim gestured with his hands, palms down. "I got some pills that can help you."

Dylan narrowed his eyes. "What kind?"

"The best, man, 2C," Tim replied.

"Woo, Woo," the three boys and Tessa shouted.

Dylan raised his eyebrows. "Where?"

"In my car."

"You know there're two officers here who are going to arrest you when this is over?" he said to Tim. "Don't you know drugs are illegal? Heh heh." His laugh was creepy.

Becca had her arms around Kelly to steady her. The two police officers glanced at each other.

———◆———

In a similar situation a few months before, Jason had been held hostage with several others in a bank robbery and had to give up his gun then too. Unlike Dylan, the perpetrator in the bank was nervous and shaky. He didn't know about guns and took a shot at someone who tried to leave. Luckily, the gun jammed, and Jason saw an opportunity. Tackling the thief, he was able to get the gun and handcuff the suspect.

Analyzing the current situation Jason watched Dylan, who was surprisingly steady and held the gun as though he were an expert. Dylan had to have had training in shooting a weapon. Jason observed the trigger was dead center, ready to shoot. Jason's trained mind thought of every scenario. Startling or attacking Dylan was not a good idea. Making sure no one got hurt was his main concern. What could he say to Dylan to make him surrender the gun? Tim mentioning drugs to Dylan was a smart move. It might entice him to leave the cafeteria for the drugs, knowing the SWAT team would soon be arriving.

"If you give us the gun now, we can work something out. We don't want to see anyone hurt," Jason pleaded.

Dylan pointed the gun at Jason and shook his head.

"Hey, tall dude, *I'm* interested in your pills." Tessa spoke up. "Hey, Dylan, can we leave?" she asked, indicating her and Tim.

"Nobody's leaving." Dylan pointed the gun at Tessa. "You stupid bitch, you know you're talking about drugs in front of two cops."

"You're holding a gun. I thought you were gonna shoot them," she said.

Dylan's face became distorted. He narrowed his eyes, his face turned red, and the veins in his neck bulged. Beads of sweat were forming on his forehead. "Shut up before I shoot you too."

———◆———

Michael could tell the situation was dire. He saw the two police officers looking at each other. He saw Becca hold onto Kelly while she rubbed her arm and whispered in her ear. He imagined she was trying to console her. Lorraine sat there like a puppy dog admiring her master, while Tessa and the three boys were being their usual asshole selves. Michael thought, once again, that Dylan was terrifying and bullying *even* the police officers.

Day after day, these low-life dipshits picked away at my dignity like they had nothing else to do. They sent emails, Instagram photos, texts. They even put a picture of me on Facebook picking up my lunch off the floor with my teeth. The next day, kids I like even made fun of me. They did the same thing to poor Kelly. That pervert over there, Ethan, tried to feel her up in biology. It scared the shit out of her. I wanted to help, but I knew they would gang up on me too. But I have a chance now. I can make things right.

He had to think of something.

Michael sat next to Kelly at the end of the table. Dylan stood next to the police officers. Occasionally, he paced behind him and Kelly pointing the gun. Thoughts swam in his head.

Something has to be done soon or Dylan will become impatient and shoot someone. What, what?

His thoughts were disturbed when Officer Regino said, "You know the SWAT team is probably here by now. If you give me the gun, we can leave peacefully. No harm done."

Michael thought the officer tried his best to make Dylan give him the gun, but it only infuriated him more.

CHAPTER 26

Becca could see Dylan getting angrier as Jason tried to convince him to give up the gun. Even though she herself was frightened, Becca did her best to calm Kelly, who cried as her entire body shook. Dylan walked back and forth like a tiger. Holding that gun, he was unpredictable. Jason and Officer Hastings looked at each other and appeared helpless. Becca empathized with Jason. *What can he do?* She thought about talking to Dylan herself but wanted to make sure she didn't anger him. Even his friends had a look of concern on their faces. "Dylan," she called.

Dylan turned to look at Becca. "What!" he growled, his anger rising.

"Kelly is getting sick. Do you think we can let her leave?"

"NO! Tell that skanky bitch to shut up. She's pissing me off."

Kelly whimpered, and Becca put her arm around her shoulder to comfort her.

Again Becca said, "Dylan." This time he didn't say anything. He just glared at her. "I don't think you want to hurt any of us." She shook her head imploring him. "We can't stay here all day. I know you didn't plan to grab the gun. If you give it back to the officer, they'll say you willingly gave it up, and you won't be in too much trouble."

Dylan took one hand off the gun to wipe the sweat from his forehead. "Oh, you know the law, huh? You don't think I'll be in *trouble*?" He paced nervously back and forth as he talked. "Girl… I'm in a shit load of trouble. Can you help me with that?"

"No," Jason spoke up. "She can't help you, but I can."

"How? What can you do?" Dylan's breathing was heavy. His body twitched.

"I can say you saw the gun almost fall out of the officer's holster and… you caught it before it discharged." Jason was grasping at straws. Becca knew he would say anything to make Dylan give up the gun. Jason continued. "If the gun had gone off, it could've hurt someone."

Dylan took a deep breath. "You would say that?"

"Sure, I don't want anyone getting hurt, including you."

Becca prayed Jason was convincing.

Jason locked eyes with Tim knowing his hands were under the table ready to draw his gun. He gave a slight shake of his head to alert Tim to wait. Drawing his gun would cause panic, and Dylan might accidentally discharge the gun, possibly killing someone. No, the only way was to talk him into giving him the gun no matter what false promises Jason had to make.

When Mrs. Franklin heard the news of the hostages, she called Eric. He left the office immediately and arrived shortly before the SWAT team. Eric met her at the door as she waited for them to arrive.

When the SWAT team arrived, they were ready to enter the lunchroom as soon as the captain's orders were given. First, he gave orders for the students to remain in their classrooms with their teachers. All the administrators, including Mrs. Franklin were asked to remain in their offices.

The school was now in lockdown. All the students were safely ushered to classrooms and hunkered down to wait for further instructions.

Eric was lucky he was able to enter the building before the lockdown. "What are the plans for saving these kids?" Eric said to Mrs. Franklin as both waited in her office. "I talked Becca into this assignment, and now she and the others are being held hostage."

"I spoke to the captain and requested he wait and let Officer Regino retrieve the gun peacefully. He said he would wait only a few more minutes," Mrs. Franklin said with a worried expression on her face.

"The SWAT team is stationed outside the lunchroom where the door is slightly ajar. Fortunately, from their angle they can see the group huddled around a table with Dylan waving the gun. Dylan is too busy concentrating on his hostages and can't see them.

"They've been in there for twenty minutes," Mrs. Franklin told Eric as she looked at her watch. "Dylan has such a bad reputation for violence. I hope Officer Regino can talk him into giving up the gun. There's no telling what he'll do. I'm afraid if the SWAT team goes in, he might shoot"—her voice trailed off and she placed her hand to her chest—"and harm someone."

"How long do you think the SWAT team holds off?" Eric asked.

Mrs. Franklin didn't respond. She shrugged and closed her eyes tightly.

———◆———

Michael twitched in his seat while listening to what Officer Regino was telling Dylan. *Does he believe that? Even I don't believe it. I know Dylan is not the sharpest tool in the shed, but I don't think even he believes the officer. But it was a good try.* Michael sized up the situation. He knew Dylan was angry when he grabbed the gun. He only wanted to get even with the lady officer, but it escalated into holding them hostage. Michael knew it was a matter of time before the SWAT team came in. He had an idea. Michael watched Dylan walk back and forth as he eyed everyone. *Maybe I can trip him when he walks near me.* Michael believed that was the only logical thing to do. *I have to do it quickly. I can't linger, or he may suspect.* Michael sat up straight in his seat and tilted his body to give himself enough room to put out his foot the next time Dylan passed him. *I have to do it just right. If I fail, he'll probably shoot me.*

"So what do you say, Dylan? You want to give me the gun so we can all leave safely?" Jason's voice was strong and convincing.

"How can I believe you?" Dylan removed his left hand from the gun to push back his hair that had fallen in his face, and then wiped his forehead before placing it back on the gun.

"Listen, we're not all saints, right?" Jason looked at Officer Hastings. She nodded her head. "I got in some trouble when I was your age. And a very nice police officer helped me too."

"What kind of trouble?" Dylan snarled.

"In high school I beat up a kid. He called me names. The cop that broke up the fight talked to me and helped me. He impressed me. That's why I became a cop."

Dylan stared at Jason and continued the pacing he'd done for the past half hour. As Dylan walked towards Michael, his plan unfolded.

Quickly, he stuck his foot out and, as planned, tripped Dylan. Caught off balance, Dylan fell. Michael immediately jumped on him to try to get the gun. Simultaneously, both officers reacted and rushed towards Dylan and Michael. When Michael struggled with Dylan for the gun, it fired a bullet that ricocheted off the leg of the next table, bounced up and, ironically, landed in the seat of the chair that Tim had previously occupied before he became one of the hostages.

As Tim stood ready, Officer Hastings pulled Michael off Dylan. Jason immediately grabbed the gun and quickly handed it to her. He placed handcuffs on Dylan and pulled him to his feet, carefully removing the gun Dylan had placed in his pants.

***

The SWAT team stormed in when Michael tripped Dylan, and within minutes, everything was under control. Dylan, in handcuffs, was lead out of the lunchroom. They detained the other students, including Becca, to determine that no other weapons were involved and to make sure no one else was injured. Tim Calloway was treated as one of the students so his identity wasn't revealed.

Becca and Jason praised Michael for his heroic deed. "You know you took a chance when you tripped him," Jason said as he placed a hand on Michael's shoulder.

"It was the only thing I could do," Michael said, shaking his head. "I thought about it and knew he wasn't going to give you the gun."

"Well, all I can say is… man, you were brave in there. You saved our lives." Jason squeezed Michael's shoulder then removed his hand and guided Michael, Becca, and Kelly, who could hardly stand, out of the cafeteria. "Okay, let's go face the music."

Becca led Kelly to the paramedics who waited outside the cafeteria. She told them Kelly should go to the emergency room for a checkup because she was so badly shaken.

"We'll take good care of her," said the paramedic. "Mike, see if her parents are behind the line," he told his associate.

Mike asked, "What's her name?"

"Kelly Richards." Becca said then turned to hug Kelly. "Don't worry. They'll take good care of you. I'm sure your parents are outside. I'll call you tonight."

Kelly nodded. Unsteady on her feet, the paramedic led her out of the building while his associate went looking for her parents. When Becca saw Eric, she walked over to him. Putting her hands to her face, she started to cry. He held her for a few seconds before she gently pulled away and wiped her eyes.

"Are you okay? I never would have let you do this if I knew something like this would happen," Eric said sadly.

"I never thought it would get this bad," she said, wiping her eyes and shaking her head.

"She did a great job in there." Jason told Eric when he came to stand with them. He put his arm around Becca's shoulder. "I'm really proud of you." He turned to Eric. "She kept her cool." Becca looked up at Jason and gave him a warm smile. He wiped a tear from her eye. Eric looked at them and raised an eyebrow.

"Thanks for protecting the kids." Eric put his hand out toward Jason.

"Just doing my job," Jason said as he removed his arm from Becca's shoulder to shake Eric's hand.

One of the SWAT team members came over and said, "I'm sorry, miss, you'll have to come down to the precinct to answer some questions."

"I'm her lawyer. I'm coming too," Eric said.

The officer nodded his head in acknowledgement. Becca and the others had to go in for questioning. Jason said he would be going as well.

"I hope Kelly will be okay," Becca said. "I'll call her when I get home tonight. I'll be able to give her mother more information." Becca looked at Eric. "I'm sure she wants to know how we'll proceed with the law suit."

"I'll know more after the questioning."

Before they left for the police station, they waited as the SWAT team ushered the children out one class at a time. Their parents waited behind the yellow tape shouting the names of their children. Even though the police tried to keep order, it was total chaos.

———◆———

Becca's parents waited patiently, hoping to see her walk out. The news had traveled quickly over radio and television. Becca's father heard it first then called his wife, and within no time, they were at the scene behind the yellow tape. All that was reported was several kids and two police officers were being held hostage at gunpoint. No one could tell them if she was one of the hostages. No names had been released.

When she finally emerged with Eric, Jason, and a member of the SWAT team, they breathed a sigh of relief, grateful that she was safe and unharmed. Becca spotted her parents and waved. She nodded her head to let them know she was fine. They waved back from behind the yellow tape, and Becca made a gesture with her hand to her ear indicating she would call.

Dylan's crew was taken to police headquarters in two squad cars. Under arrest, Dylan was taken alone in another car. Jason drove Michael, Becca, and Eric in his. Becca sat in the back seat with Eric. Michael sat next to Jason. They explained to Michael that Becca was Kelly's Guardian ad Litem. Surprised, he started to ask questions.

Eric put up his hands. "Wait, I have to know the details of the hostage situation for our case."

Becca started to describe the ordeal. Whenever she missed an important point, Jason corrected her. "Oh yes, things were happening so fast, I forgot that," said Becca.

"It's my job to remember everything. I'll have to make a report." He looked at her in the rear view mirror and winked. She smiled back.

DRIVING BACK TO THE PRECINCT, Jason thought about the seriousness of the hostage situation. Even though he winked at Becca trying to lighten the mood, he realized they all could have been killed. The thought of Becca being harmed sent a stabbing pain to his heart. With all the tension going on in that room, all he could think about was saving those kids, but most of all, saving Becca. Over these last few days, she had become very precious to him. He knew he was beginning to care deeply for her.

"What kind of questions will they ask?" Michael said breaking Jason's thoughts.

"Becca will have to explain that she was there in a Guardian ad Litem position to help Kelly because of the bullying. She's also a witness to Dylan's actions. They'll ask Becca and you some preliminary questions about how Dylan was able to pull the gun from Officer Hastings. Of course, I'll have to give a full report as well as Officer Hastings. Dylan will be fingerprinted and have mug shots taken. He's definitely going to spend some time in Juvie. He will *not* be returning to that school."

"Well, we'll certainly have enough material to sue, on Kelly's behalf, for the abuse she received from those kids. It was evident," Jason said, nodding to Becca.

———————

At headquarters, Michael was taken to a room for questioning. Becca and Jason were taken into another room. Eric was there as her lawyer, and Jason as a supporting witness. It lasted for a little more than an hour.

Becca rubbed her temples. She was completely exhausted. "Where's Michael? Will he be in trouble for tackling Dylan? What's going to happen to him?"

"Wait here," said Jason. "I'll find out." He walked out of the room.

Eric addressed the questioning officer. "Are we done here? If we are, we'll wait outside."

The officer told Becca that she was done for now, however, she may be called again for further questioning. They walked out of the room to wait for Jason.

"Becca, I know you're tired. Why don't I take you home? We can wait to hear about Michael later. I'm sure your parents are worried," Eric said, watching Becca rub her eyes.

Becca opened her mouth and made the sound people make when they forget something. "Oh no, I have to call them." She pulled out her phone.

She called her dad and assured him she was fine. As she suspected, he was full of questions. She told him she would explain everything when she got home.

As she hung up, Jason walked over. "Michael's parents are with him. They're totally distraught. Happy that he's alive, angry for what he did, sad that he was a victim of bullying. I've seen it before. They don't know which way to turn. I told them that he was actually a hero and saved all our lives. I don't think he'll be in any trouble, but he does need an attorney." Jason faced Eric. "I mentioned that you were here as Becca's attorney. They asked if you would talk to them."

"Go, Eric, I can wait here for you."

"But, Becca, your parents are worried."

"Don't worry," said Jason, "I can take her home."

Eric nodded his head. "Is that okay with you, Becca? If I'm going to help the kid, I have to do it now."

Becca was so exhausted. She shook her head and looked at Jason then at Eric. "Please help him. He's a good kid."

"I'll do my best," Eric said. Jason pointed and told him where to find them.

As they walked to Jason's squad car Becca said, "All I want to do is go home, eat a good meal, and take a shower." Becca couldn't think anymore.

———

Jason knew Becca was beat and occasionally turned to glance at her during the drive. Her eyes were closed and her head rested on the seat. Every once in a while she would sigh.

He didn't want to disturb her. She looked so peaceful. The last several hours had been frightening and unpredictable.

Becca opened her eyes, sat up in the seat, and turned to Jason. "What's going to happen to those kids? What about Michael?"

"I'm sure Eric will do whatever it takes to help him. He seems to be a compassionate person and a competent lawyer. Michael will be lucky to have him as his attorney. As far as the other kids, they'll probably have detention and possibly be expelled. We know what's going to happen to Dylan."

"Michael was so brave when he tripped Dylan," Becca said looking at Jason.

"He sure was. He went a step beyond when he tried to grab the gun. I know Eric will help with that. He put his own life in jeopardy to save all of us," Jason said then turned to Becca and smiled. "This incident should shake people up. You wanted to help with the bullying. I believe you have. Think about that. Think about how you helped Kelly."

She put her head back again and closed her eyes. Speaking in a low voice, almost to herself, she said, "Yes, poor kid. I must call her when I get home. How can I help her get through this?"

They drove quietly for the rest of the ride. Jason admired this lovely, brave young woman. He wanted to be in her life and felt compelled to protect her any way he could. He knew she was worried about explaining the day to her parents. Should he ask if she wanted his help to explain? He let her rest, hoping she would ask.

CHAPTER 28

WHEN THEY ARRIVED AT THE house, Becca was still asleep. Jason didn't want to wake her; she looked so peaceful. He wished he could wake her with a kiss. Then Becca blinked her eyes a few times to wake up. She stretched one arm over her shoulder then looked at Jason. "Was I asleep the whole time?"

"Most of it," he said, nodding.

"I thought I dreamt the whole thing. I wished I did," Becca said looking deeply into Jason's eyes. Now exhausted, strands of hair loosened from her ponytail fell on her cheeks. He gently tucked the strands behind her ear, fighting a strong desire to embrace her and tell her how he really felt.

Just as he was about to say something, the front door to her house flung open; her parents rushed to the patrol car.

"Are you alright," her mother said peeking into the passenger window. Becca's father was behind her bending over her mother's shoulder.

Becca opened the car door. "I'm fine. I'm fine," she said and hugged both of them.

"We want to hear all about it," said her mother.

Jason got out of the vehicle and walked around to greet her parents. "She was wonderful. You both should be proud of her."

"We were proud of her before this ordeal started," said Becca's father.

"Officer, would you like to come in and let us know what happened?" Becca's mother asked.

"Yes, I would be happy to," Jason said, thinking his wish had come true.

They walked into the house with Becca's parents hugging her on both sides.

Inside their living room, Jason proceeded to tell her parents what had happened in the cafeteria. They both listened intensely, occasionally looking at each other. When he came to the part about Dylan pulling the gun, her mother held her hand to her mouth and gasped. Becca didn't interfere. She listened to him explain their terrible ordeal. Occasionally he glanced at her. There was a glimmer of light in her eyes that made him hopeful.

When he finished the story, Becca's mother offered Jason something to eat. "You must be hungry and just as exhausted as Becca."

"Actually, I am, Mrs. Curtis. Thank you very much. We didn't have time for lunch."

For the first time, the four of them laughed.

———◆———

They went into the kitchen and continued to talk while Becca's mother prepared some sandwiches and tea.

While they were eating, Becca's cell phone rang. It was Eric. He told her that Michael was released to his parents. He didn't think he would be charged with anything after Becca and Jason had given their statements, hailing Michael a hero.

"I'm so happy to hear that. As soon as I finish eating and take a shower, I'm going to call Kelly. Maybe go over to see her," Becca told Eric.

"That's a great idea," Eric said. "I'm heading back to the office to prepare for our lawsuit. Please ask Mrs. Richards if they can meet us at the office tomorrow at ten a.m. I know it's Saturday, but I want to get a head start on the case before Monday."

———◆———

"Mr. and Mrs. Curtis, I'm sorry to eat and run." Jason stood. "Thank you for your hospitality. I'm heading back to the precinct. I have to return the patrol car." Jason turned to Becca. "My shift ends in half an hour. If you want me to take you to the Richards' house, I'd be happy to."

"Oh…yes, yes that would be great." Becca stood and hugged him. He felt something stirring inside and knew he was falling for her.

Becca's mother walked Jason to the door and thanked him for helping her daughter.

"It was my pleasure, ma'am. I'll see you later."

Becca's mother stood by the door as Jason walked to his patrol car. She waited for him to pull out before she closed the door then walked back into the kitchen.

Becca was on the phone telling Mrs. Richards that she and Jason would stop by later to see Kelly. When she hung up, her mother said with a sigh, "My, my, that boy is such a catch."

"Mother!" Becca was surprised to hear her say that.

"Well, I see the way you both look at each other. It's obvious to me how you both feel." She glanced at her husband while she spoke. He nodded his head in approval.

"Daddy! You too? It's just professional. We had an assignment together. But I must admit having Jason in that cafeteria made me feel safe. I should shower before he gets back." The three laughed and hugged each other, grateful the ordeal was over.

Jason returned to the precinct and changed into civilian clothes. He glanced in the mirror and rubbed his light beard. *Not bad.* He combed his hair and splashed on cologne. He wanted to make sure he looked his best.

As he was leaving, he bumped into Tim Calloway.

"Wow, that was close," Tim said as he wiped he brow.

"Yeah. That kid was so unpredictable; the gun was chambered and ready to shoot," Jason said shaking his head. "I had to keep talking to him to get his mind off killing someone."

"You did a great job," said Tim. "By the way, did you know that before I moved over to the table, I was sitting in the seat where the bullet landed?"

"Wow, no…I didn't know that. Man… that was one way to say your ass was on the line." They both laughed and continued to talk about the case. Jason told him what he heard from Eric about Michael, and Tim was glad. "He's a good kid. Talk about asses, he actually saved ours. Well, I gotta go. I'm taking Becca to Kelly Richards' house to talk to her parents about the case."

"Hmm," said Tim. I saw the way you looked at Becca. She's hot. You got something going on?"

"No…no, but I do like her. Is it that obvious?"

"Well, if you don't ask her out, I will," Tim said as he landed a soft punch to Jason's shoulder.

"As a matter of fact, I plan on it. I better get going. I don't want to be late." Jason winked at Tim and returned a slightly harder punch to *his* shoulder.

"Ow." Tim said as he rubbed his shoulder. "I get the message."

<hr>

While Becca showered and dressed, she recalled the events of the day. *Is it that obvious how I feel about Jason? He was so brave with Dylan. He told me later that Dylan had triggered the gun and was ready to shoot. I'm glad he didn't tell my parents. They don't know about guns and think they all have safeties. That's why the gun went off when Michael jumped Dylan.*

She continued dressing, making sure she wore something that would capture Jason's eye. She looked in the mirror and said aloud, "Yes, Mom and Dad are right; I'm definitely falling for Jason. I hope he feels the same."

CHAPTER 29

———◆———

JASON GOT INTO HIS PERSONAL vehicle and glanced at the time. Forty-five minutes had passed since he left Becca's house. *I hope I gave her enough time to shower and change. Tim is right I do like her…a lot! I hope she feels the same. He did notice the way we both look at each other.*

He continued thinking of the events of the day, and that luckily no one was hurt. *It could have been disastrous. I'm so glad Michael isn't in trouble. It's kids like Dylan that give teenagers a bad name. I hope Eric throws the book at him.*

He arrived at Becca's house in record time. He couldn't wait to see her again.

Mrs. Curtis opened the door. "Hello, Jason. Come in. She's almost ready." She greeted him with a warm smile that made him feel welcome. "You look nice in your civilian clothes."

"Thank you, ma'am."

"Ditto that," Becca said as she walked into the room.

"Thanks." Jason widened his eyes. "I must say the same about you. You look great."

With a smile of approval, Becca's mother glanced at them showing she was pleased. "What time will you be coming home? Should we wait for you to have dinner?"

Before Becca could answer, Jason said. "That's okay; we'll grab something after we leave Kelly's."

Becca tilted her head. She and her mother looked at each other, raising their eyebrows.

"I'm sorry. Is that okay with you, Becca?" Jason realized he was taking liberty. He was used to being in control.

"Oh…no, no that would be fine." Becca said as she turned toward her mother.

"Okay, we won't wait. Enjoy your dinner," said her mother.

***

After Becca and Jason left, Mrs. Curtis closed the door and turned to her husband. "He reminds me of you, the bossy type," she said, laughing.

"I beg your pardon," her husband said. "I always thought you were the boss."

They both laughed. "I think they make a lovely couple," said Becca's mother.

"Now, Marion, don't go playing cupid. Becca has to make up her own mind about who she dates."

"I know, but they do look good together," her mother said with a sigh.

———•———

Jason and Becca chatted as they drove to the Richards' home. "I wonder how much Kelly told her parents," Becca said. "She was in and out of consciousness most of the time. She kept fainting and crying. How much should I tell her parents?" Becca glanced at Jason.

"Well, if Eric is going to try this case, I think they should know everything," said Jason. "But for tonight, let's keep it light. They'll find out more when Eric meets with them."

Becca nodded, agreeing with him. "I'm just going to focus on the fact that it ended well."

"Are you worried, Becca?" Jason asked.

"No…not as long as you're with me." She blushed.

"I'll be with you, as long as it takes," he said, hoping she realized that he cared for her. When she looked at him and smiled, he felt she did.

———•———

They arrived at Kelly's two-story Key West style house, very neatly landscaped. Mrs. Richards answered the door and was glad to see them. Becca introduced her to Jason. "This is Officer Jason Regino. He was in the cafeteria with us."

Mrs. Richards nodded and shook his hand. "Please come in." She directed them to the living room, comfortably decorated with a rust-colored sofa and love seat. A table against the wall was adorned with family portraits, most were of Kelly. Plantation shutters covered the large window allowing the sun to enter the room. Fresh flowers were placed on the coffee table. In the corner of the room was a bookcase filled with novels and history and biology books.

"Kelly is resting in her bedroom. The doctor gave her a mild sedative. Make yourselves comfortable, and I'll get her. She'll be happy to see you."

"Are you sure it's okay to disturb her?" Becca asked. "I heard the news media tried to question her at the hospital. They were all over us at the precinct."

"Oh no, we got rid of them quickly. She's been asking to see you." Mrs. Richards left the room to get Kelly.

"See, Becca," Jason said, "she considers you her friend."

"Some friend; I almost got her killed in a hostage situation."

"Don't think of it that way," Kelly's father said as he walked into the room.

Becca and Jason were shocked to hear him say that. Jason stood to shake his hand. "Hello, Mr.

Richards. I'm Officer Jason Regino, and this is Becca Curtis."

"Please, call me Jim." He walked over to shake Becca's hand too. "So this is the famous Becca that Kelly talks about non-stop." As usual, Becca gripped his hand. "Firm grip, young lady. That tells me a lot about you."

Becca looked at Jason. Her furrowed brow indicated surprise. Jason nodded his head in agreement with Jim Richards.

"Ever since Kelly met you, Becca, she's begun to come alive again. Her mother and I thought you were the answer to our prayers. She had been so despondent since the bullying began. Kelly is an intellectual, however, not strong willed. She let the situation get the best of her."

"But, Mr. Richards…Jim, I thought the hostage situation would set her way back."

"She was very much disturbed by it, but she was more concerned for your safety and that young man, Michael. According to Kelly, he's a hero."

"Yes, he saved all of us," Becca said.

"That he did," Jason nodded.

"Her only words all day were, 'I want to see Becca.'"

Becca sat up in her seat. "I'm honored. I've been very worried about her too."

Kelly entered the room with her mother and ran over to Becca. They hugged each other. "I'm so happy to see you." Then she wobbled a bit. Becca held onto her.

Kelly's mother grabbed her too. "It's the sedative. Here, sit next to Becca." She guided her daughter to the seat.

Kelly looked at Jason and in a weak voice said, "You're the officer in the cafeteria? Why aren't you wearing your uniform?"

"Yes, I am. I'm off duty, and I wanted to come to see how you're doing."

"Is Michael okay?" She covered her eyes with her hands and started to cry.

Becca put her arm around her shoulder as she did in the cafeteria. "It's okay, Kelly, you can cry." Kelly glanced up, and Becca knew she would see the tears in her own eyes.

"We're here to tell you that we're going to see that those kids never bother you again," Jason said with conviction.

"The corners of Kelly's mouth began to form a smile." Her mother and father looked at each other and smiled too.

Lovingly, with her arm still around Kelly's shoulder, Becca spoke in a tender voice, "We don't want you to worry about being bullied ever again. My firm, and Jason and I"—she nodded in his direction—"are making sure of it. We want you to rest for the next few days while school is out. When you return, you'll be a new person, *free* from bullying. Eric Jefferies is going to see that those bullies are stopped."

A wider smile appeared on Kelly's face. "I trust and believe you."

"After all," Becca said, "you're now *on eagle's wings*."

Kelly nodded and smiled, remembering the quote that Becca stated throughout their ordeal.

"I love it," said Becca, "and always felt safe when I said it. Now, I'm passing it on to you."

Kelly slowly began to recite the song.

After she finished, Becca said, "You see, Kelly, as long as you believe, you'll always be on eagle's wings." The two hugged each other.

Kelly's mother wiped tears from her eyes. "I know you were her Guardian ad Litem, but to me you were her *guardian angel.* Kelly told us how you looked after her."

"Thank you, it was my pleasure," Becca gave Kelly a squeeze, "I've grown to care for this cutie. I'll always be her guardian angel."

Jason had a wide smile on his face, as did Kelly's father.

"Jim"—Becca turned to him—"Eric Jefferies wanted to know if you and your wife will be able to come into the office tomorrow to sign some documents so we can get the procedure started. Even though it's Saturday, he'll make an exception in your case."

"Of course, what time does he want us there?"

"How is ten o'clock?"

"Fine, we'll see him at ten. Will you be there?"

"Of course." She gave Kelly another squeeze.

Jason stood; it was time to leave. "Goodbye." Jason nodded to Kelly. "Mr. Richards." He extended his hand to him and his wife. "Mrs. Richards."

Becca hugged Kelly and told her she would see her the next day, and would come to visit again before school started.

When Becca put her hand out to Mr. and Mrs. Richards, instead of shaking it, they both hugged her with tears in their eyes.

"WHERE WOULD YOU LIKE TO go for dinner?" Jason asked as they drove away from Kelly's house. "Do you like Outback?"

"Hmm?" Becca responded.

"I said, do you like Outback." Jason looked over at her and realized she was in deep thought.

Becca turned to Jason and blinked as if to clear her mind. "Oh, yes, I like Outback."

"Good. There's one a few blocks from here. I thought we could go there."

Becca nodded her head but didn't say a word.

"What's up? Do you want to talk about it?"

"I can't believe what happened today. I feel like it was a dream, actually a nightmare." Becca turned again toward Jason as she spoke.

Jason touched her hand that was laying on the armrest. "It *was* a nightmare, but not a dream; it was real." He turned to look at her. "I'm so grateful that no one was hurt, especially you."

She placed her right hand on his and smiled.

Jason continued to drive, content with her hand on his. When he reached the restaurant, he was surprised the parking lot was empty. *Good, it will be quiet inside and we can talk.*

When they entered the restaurant Becca said, "Oh good; it's not crowded."

"Yeah, I'm glad. This place is always jammed," said Jason.

The hostess led them to a booth in the back. When Becca sat, she sighed. "What a day. Reality is starting to set in. When I think of what could have happened…" she said, her voice trailing off.

"I know how you feel, but you have to put it past you and think about the outcome, and how it will benefit both Kelly and Michael. Isn't that what you wanted?" Jason had both hands out, palms up.

Becca nodded. A slight smile formed in the corners of her mouth. She squeezed one of his outstretched hands. "I don't know if I could have gone through it without you being there." He squeezed back.

"Do you know what Eric's plans are for tomorrow?" Jason said, still holding her hand.

"Without too many gory details, he's going to explain to the Richards what happened. With yours, mine, and Officer Hastings' corroboration, we should have a good law suit against the parents of those bullies."

"That tall kid should testify as well," said Becca.

Jason was not allowed to tell her that Tim was undercover. Even though he didn't want to keep any secrets from her, it was his duty as an officer. "Oh yes, I'm sure they questioned him at the station."

"Jason, do you think you can come into the office tomorrow?"

"Yes I can, as long as you agree to spend the rest of the day with me."

"Aren't you working tomorrow?"

"No, I have the entire weekend off, and I'm looking forward to spending most of it with you."

Becca put her head down and blushed.

Jason realized he was moving too fast. He'd never met anyone like Becca. He was quite impressed with her. Up until now, his waking thoughts were of his position on the force and his plans for advancement. Although there were many attractive and eligible women on the job, he never allowed himself the luxury to date any of them. Now, all he could think of was Becca. "Sorry, am I taking liberties again?"

"No…no, I never experienced someone who was so…so…"

"Honest and forward." He finished her sentence.

"Yes, see what I mean, you even finish my sentences."

"I'm sorry; I guess it's my vocation."

The waitress came over to take their drink order. Jason wanted to tell Becca to order a glass of wine but realized he was being a little too pushy. "What would you like, Becca?"

"I think I'd like a glass of Merlot."

Jason smiled. *She read my mind.*

Becca looked at the menu and asked, "What's good here, Jason."

Okay, she asked me. "Well, I like the Alice Springs Chicken. But there are many good items on the menu."

"Sounds good, I think I'll have that too."

After they ordered their food, Jason held up his wine glass and said, "To better days."

Becca tapped his glass with hers and said, "I'll drink to that."

They talked a little about the case but mostly about themselves. Becca told Jason how much she loved the law and was eager to pass the bar and become a practicing attorney. He confessed that he eventually wanted to work towards being a detective. They chatted about their childhood and their desire to marry and have a family.

"When I get married, I want at least three children," Becca said. "It was lonely being an only child."

"How would you like to grow up in a household of four?" Jason told her about his siblings. He had two brothers and one sister.

"Wow, I feel sorry for your sister, thrown into all that testosterone."

"Nah, she was the oldest and got to boss us around."

Their conversation went on long after they finished their meal. Becca clicked on her cell phone and saw that it was past nine o'clock. "You won't believe what time it is."

"I guess we should be going. I know you have a big day tomorrow," Jason said as he looked at his phone.

They left the restaurant, and Jason casually held her hand as they walked to the car.

When Jason pulled into Becca's driveway, he shut the motor off. He wanted to kiss her but she indicated earlier that he was forward, so he turned to look at her. "I had a wonderful evening. I enjoy spending time with you and look forward to the weekend. I really like you, Becca." He left her to guide the moment.

"I like you too, Jason, and I had a wonderful time as well, considering the crazy day we had." She put her hand to her head as though remembering the ordeal.

Jason felt the need to protect her and instinctively put his arm around her and drew her to his chest. She looked up at him and, all too naturally, they kissed.

After the kiss, they both stared into each other's eyes, and Becca gently drew away. "Thanks again. I'll see you tomorrow in my office at ten. Then we can plan on doing something fun…for a change."

Jason laughed. "Yes, I promise. Get a good night's sleep." He watched her walk to the front door and lingered after she went in. *I'm going to marry that girl.*

CHAPTER 31

———◆———

BOTH HER PARENTS WERE WATCHING the ten o'clock news when Becca came home. Her mother shouted from the living room, "How did it go? How's Kelly?"

Becca went into the living room, and her father lowered the television. "It went very well. I had a pleasant conversation with Kelly even though she was slightly sedated. Her parents are great and so appreciative of all we're doing for their daughter. Eric wants to meet with them at ten a.m. tomorrow."

"Tomorrow? It's Saturday," said her father. "Will you be there?"

"Yes, and so will Jason. Eric wants to get as much information as he can to proceed with the case on Monday."

"Mmm," said her mother. "Jason too?"

"Yes. Eric is representing Michael as well. He and his parents will be there too."

"You know," said her father, the incident was on the news. They didn't mention any of the kids' names, but said one of them was a hero and helped stop a very serious situation."

"Oh, did they mention that I was Kelly's Guardian ad Litem?"

"No, they just said a student was able to grab an officer's gun and held two officers and several students hostage. It was mentioned that one of the hostages bravely tackled the boy."

"Oh, good," said Becca. "That's why Eric has to move fast before the news media gets out of control."

"How was your dinner with Jason?" said her mother. "I like him. I think you do too."

"Yes, he's very nice. I may spend some time with him over the weekend."

Both her parents looked at each other and smiled but didn't say anything.

"I am so exhausted," said Becca. "I need to get some rest. We'll talk more tomorrow after our meeting in the office."

Getting ready for bed, Becca recalled everything that happened that day. She wondered if there was something she could have done to change the outcome. No. She had no idea Dylan would do what he did. *Come to think of it, neither did he.* Dylan merely saw an opportunity and grabbed the gun.

She thought about the dinner with Jason. It was so romantic. She couldn't believe that in so short a time, she could have such feelings for someone. So much had happened since Mr. Jefferies died. She sat on the bed and shrugged. *I really need to get some rest. Tomorrow will be a busy day.*

Just then her cell phone rang. She hurried to pick it up so as not to disturb her parents. When she looked at the caller ID, she saw Jason's name. "Hi, Jason."

"Hi," he said. "I just wanted to hear your voice."

"But I just left you a half hour ago."

"I know. I suddenly got a stabbing pain thinking that the situation at the school could have ended differently."

"But it didn't. And we're all so happy about that."

"I was just thinking that when the meeting is over, we can go on a picnic in the park or anything else you would like to do," said Jason.

Becca was so drained, but a picnic sounded great. That's what she needed, something quiet and relaxing. "Wow, a picnic sounds nice."

"We can go over to that café near the office and pick up a few tuna sandwiches." Jason was enthusiastic.

"Great idea." Becca was trying to sound cheery, but her voice was dragging.

"You sound tired," said Jason. "Get some rest. I just wanted to call you and suggest the picnic. I thought it would be a great way for you to unwind after the meeting."

"Yes, I *am* tired and, yes, the picnic is a great idea. I'm looking forward to it."

"Okay, I'll say goodnight. Pleasant dreams. Oh… by the way. Do you want me to pick you up tomorrow?"

Becca hadn't thought about it. "Umm…yes, yes that would be great. Pick me up at nine thirty."

"See you then. Goodnight, Becca."

"Goodnight, Jason."

When she hung up, she looked at her cell phone for several seconds. She couldn't believe what a great guy he was. In the middle of all this turmoil, he thinks of a picnic. She had to admit, it was a great idea. She thought of their kiss and her heart skipped. She shook her head. *Am I falling in love?*

She then continued her nightly ritual: brushing her teeth, washing her face, and brushing her hair. She stretched and yawned, and put on her nightshirt. *That bed never looked so good to me.* She crawled into bed. *Maybe I can have that dream where I climb up the hill and finally discover my true love!* She closed her eyes and within minutes, she was sound asleep.

ERIC MADE HEADLINES WHEN HE represented Mr. and Mrs. Richards, who sued the parents of the six students that were harassing and bullying their daughter Kelly. He won the case, which started an avalanche of parents paying more attention to the activities of their children, either bullying or being bullied.

Dylan was sent to Juvenile Detention, awaiting placement in a facility. While he was being detained, he became extremely violent and fought with one of the security guards, resulting in a broken nose for the guard. This added to his sentence. The psychology professionals who examined him concluded he was a product of his home environment, where his father constantly beat him and his mother. It was only a matter of time before his violence erupted, possibly resulting in murder.

Tony, Ryan and Ethan, as well as Lorraine and Tessa, were all suspended and forced by the court to go to counseling—especially Tessa, whom they felt had a tendency for violence and criminal behavior. Lorraine's problem was her obsession with Dylan. She had low self-esteem and co-dependent tendencies.

A few of their parents were unaware of their children's bullying. Unfortunately, while working to help support the family was a priority, the behavior of their children fell through the cracks. Fortunately, the lawsuit opened their eyes to their priorities.

Kelly slowly came back to being herself, her grades picked up and, with Becca's encouragement, she volunteered in a hospital where she could observe and assist with heart patients, supporting her desire to be a cardiologist. With the money Eric won in the lawsuit, her parents could now put aside enough funds to send her to medical school.

Eric became partner in the firm and took on many cases of bullying, including road rage. He believed if more people had road manners, there would be less accidents.

The school and police department touted Michael as a hero. He became very popular in school. Both he and Kelly grew to become close friends and worked together on many school projects. Students would fight to sit with them in the lunchroom. One day when two students rushed over to get the last seat at their table, Michael, shaking his head, looked over at a beaming Kelly and said, "How ironic!" They were inseparable and their parents thought there was a romance blooming.

Becca graduated from law school and passed the bar with flying colors. She was now working as an attorney and helped Eric in his crusade against bullying. She was especially involved with his road rage cases. She would often consult with old Mr. Klein on her cases, and he was happy to assist.

Both she and Jason volunteered to speak at all the schools: elementary, middle, high school, and even some colleges. They were warmly welcomed. Now involved in cases, Becca had much more information to share with the students. Because of his expertise, Jason was assigned to all bullying cases. He also wanted to advance his career by studying to become a detective.

Seeing a lot of each other, their romance blossomed. Becca's mother thought that any day she would see a ring on her daughter's finger. Whenever Becca came home from seeing Jason, she immediately looked at her left hand. One day, teasing her mother, Becca walked in with her hands in her pockets. It had become such a habit with her mother looking for a ring. Her mother trying to be casual said, "Becca, why don't you take your jacket off."

When Jason finally did propose, Becca played a prank on her mother. Instead of putting the ring on her left hand, she placed it on her right. When she went home, as usual, her mother immediately looked at her left hand. Becca said, "Mom, are you looking for this?" and raised her right hand. Her mother put her hands to her mouth and began to cry. Becca hugged her then placed the ring on the correct finger while her mother shouted to her husband, "Our baby is engaged. It's a dream come true!"

Oh yes, Becca did have that dream again on that well-known night, and the person who beckoned her from the hill was Jason, her true love.

EDEE GREW UP IN BROOKLYN, NY and now resides in South Florida with her husband. Several years ago she studied Hypnosis, became certified, and practiced for only a short time. To better suit her clients, she wrote scripts for the hypnosis sessions. She enjoyed writing the scripts and decided to try her hand at novels. In addition to *Guardian Angel*, she has written another novel, *In Jack's Place*, many poems and two unpublished plays. Several years ago, Edee found two wonderful writers' groups in Jupiter, who nourished her love for writing and prompted her to publish and keep writing. She will be forever grateful to them. She is currently writing her third novel.

www.ingramcontent.com/pod-product-compliance
Lightning Source LLC
Chambersburg PA
CBHW031100250726
48655CB00004B/1516